GW01339574

Hawaiian History

A Captivating Guide to the History of the Big Island, Starting From Ancient Hawaii to the Present

© Copyright 2022

All Rights Reserved. No part of this book may be reproduced in any form without permission in writing from the author. Reviewers may quote brief passages in reviews.

Disclaimer: No part of this publication may be reproduced or transmitted in any form or by any means, mechanical or electronic, including photocopying or recording, or by any information storage and retrieval system, or transmitted by email without permission in writing from the publisher.

While all attempts have been made to verify the information provided in this publication, neither the author nor the publisher assumes any responsibility for errors, omissions, or contrary interpretations of the subject matter herein.

This book is for entertainment purposes only. The views expressed are those of the author alone and should not be taken as expert instruction or commands. The reader is responsible for his or her own actions.

Adherence to all applicable laws and regulations, including international, federal, state, and local laws governing professional licensing, business practices, advertising, and all other aspects of doing business in the US, Canada, UK, or any other jurisdiction, is the sole responsibility of the purchaser or reader.

Neither the author nor the publisher assumes any responsibility or liability whatsoever on behalf of the purchaser or reader of these materials. Any perceived slight of any individual or organization is purely unintentional.

Free Bonus from Captivating History (Available for a Limited time)

Hi History Lovers!

Now you have a chance to join our exclusive history list so you can get your first history ebook for free as well as discounts and a potential to get more history books for free! Simply visit the link below to join.

Captivatinghistory.com/ebook

Also, make sure to follow us on Facebook, Twitter and Youtube by searching for Captivating History.

Contents

PART 1: ANCIENT HAWAII 1
   INTRODUCTION 2
   CHAPTER 1 – THE BACKGROUND OF HAWAII 4
   CHAPTER 2 – ARRIVAL OF THE POLYNESIANS 10
   CHAPTER 3 – THE WORLD OF PRE-CONTACT HAWAII 19
   CHAPTER 4 – EUROPE MAKES CONTACT: 1778 49
   CHAPTER 5 – A PARADISE DIVIDED, AND THE WARS RAGE ON 55
   CHAPTER 6 – THE BATTLE OF NUʻUANU: 1795 70
   CHAPTER 7 – THE BIRTH OF THE KAMEHAMEHA DYNASTY: 1810 77
   CHAPTER 8 – THE END OF ANCIENT HAWAII 86
   CONCLUSION 102
PART 2: HISTORY OF HAWAII 104
   INTRODUCTION 105
   CHAPTER 1 – INTRODUCTORY OVERVIEW 107
   CHAPTER 2 – ANCIENT HAWAIʻI: THE PEOPLE OF HAWAIʻI 114
   CHAPTER 3 – ANCIENT HAWAIʻI: THE GODS AND MYTHS OF HAWAIʻI 132
   CHAPTER 4 – POINT OF CONTACT 145
   CHAPTER 5 – THE KINGDOM OF HAWAIʻI 159

CHAPTER 6 – THE UNITED STATES AND HAWAIʻI 175
CHAPTER 7 – WORLD WAR II AND HAWAIʻI 194
CHAPTER 8 – MODERN HAWAIʻI 207
CHAPTER 9 – NOTABLE PEOPLE OF HAWAIʻI 219
CHAPTER 10 – CULTURE OF HAWAIʻI 232
CONCLUSION 246
HERE'S ANOTHER BOOK BY CAPTIVATING HISTORY THAT YOU MIGHT LIKE 248
FREE BONUS FROM CAPTIVATING HISTORY (AVAILABLE FOR A LIMITED TIME) 249
REFERENCES 250

Part 1: Ancient Hawaii

A Captivating Guide to Hawaiian Human History, Starting from the Polynesian Arrival through the Growth of a Civilization to Kamehameha the Great

Introduction

Hawaii is hands-down one of the most beautiful and iconic places in the world. The archipelago of the Hawaiian Islands (also known as the Sandwich Islands) is known worldwide. With over 1.4 million people living in this natural paradise and an incredible 9.4 million tourists visiting from all over the world every year, Hawaii is a wonderland to many.

Hawaii is an archipelago consisting of over 137 islands, many of which are volcanic. Altogether, the islands span a great distance of over 1,500 miles. They are located in the heart of Oceania, and they are about two thousand miles off the western coast of the US mainland.

Although Hawaii consists of many islands, there are eight main islands that most people think of. These islands are Niʻihau, Kauaʻi, Oʻahu, Molokaʻi, Lānaʻi, Kahoʻolawe, Maui, and Hawaiʻi, with the latter also known as "Big Island" or more commonly "Hawaii Island." People who have never been to Hawaii typically think that the Big Island is the most visited island, but the truth is Oʻahu is the most visited one. (You might notice the okina in these words, which represents a glottal stop. We have decided to use the traditional spelling of the islands and rulers' names. When Hawaii is referred to in general, it will be spelled as "Hawaii.")

But this is modern-day Hawaii. You have heard about the white-sand beaches, the glorious year-round sunshine, and dominating mountain coastlines, as well as the spectacular natural wonders, stunning national parks, and awe-inspiring beauty stops. But what are the origins of such a prestigious country? What was the world of ancient Hawaii like?

Even saying the words "ancient Hawaii" sparks a certain curiosity in our minds, a spark that makes us want to dig down and see what lies below the surface. What were the people of ancient Hawaii like? What kind of culture, society, government, and religion existed here?

We are going to travel back to when the islands first started out. Read of the stories of Hawaii's rising kingdoms and falling dynasties, of gods past and present, and the perhaps inevitable transition into the modern world.

Within the following chapters, you will discover the deep and twisting story of ancient Hawaii. Experience Hawaii's trials and tribulations alongside its triumphs and tragedies. In many regards, this is Hawaii as you have never seen it before. So, sit back, relax, and dive into the captivating history of these tropical islands.

Chapter 1 – The Background of Hawaii

Before we hop into when the islands were first inhabited, it is worth taking a look at how Hawaii was formed. Many might know that the Hawaiian Islands are a group of volcanic islands. As the term "volcanic islands" suggests, these islands were created from volcanoes, and they began to be formed around forty to seventy million years ago.

Hawaii was created by hotspot volcanism. Typically, volcanoes are created by tectonic plates coming together. Hotspots, on the other hand, are in fixed spots.

To put it very simply, the islands were formed (and are still being formed) as the Pacific Plate slowly moved northwest over these fixed hot spots. The islands would pop up one after the other. In fact, there are a number of submerged mountains called seamounts in the Hawaiian archipelago.

Interestingly, the most northwestern islands are the oldest, and dating the land of the islands can show modern scientists the speed at which the Pacific Oceanic plate was moving all those years ago.

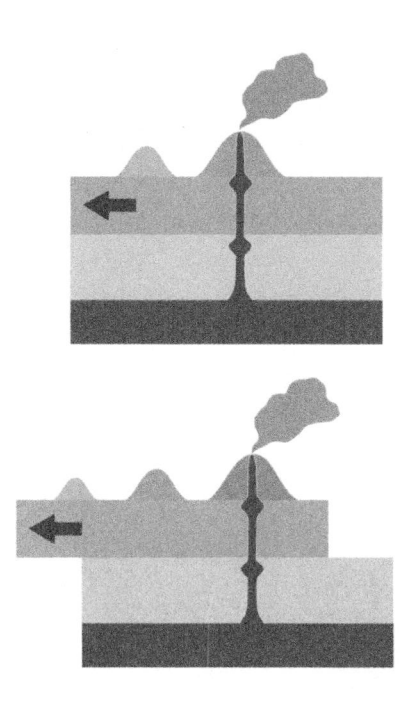

A simple diagram of how the plate moved over a hot spot and created land. (Credit: Los668; Wikimedia Commons)

Mauna Loa, the Earth's largest active volcano, can be found on the Big Island. It is one of these hotspot volcanoes. It makes up a little more than half of the island, and it stands at an impressive 13,678 feet above sea level, which makes it taller than Mount Everest! Small eruptions occur every few years, with the last significant one dating back to April 15th, 1984.

Other active volcanoes include Kīlauea and Lōʻihi. While Kīlauea is aboveground, Lōʻihi is an underwater volcano. Lōʻihi is the newest volcano in the Hawaiian region, and it will eventually rise above sea level. However, that will not happen for another 10,000 to 100,000 years! This means that the Hawaiian Islands will continue to be formed for a long time. For example, Kīlauea has been erupting off and on since 1983. Since that year, it has added around 700 acres of new land.

Hawaii's black-sand beaches are due to these volcanoes. When lava comes into contact with water, it cools. The sudden change in temperature causes the lava to shatter into sharp pieces. This means there is only so much black sand to go around, as the volcanoes are not constantly erupting. Hawaii has made it illegal to take black sand from its beaches because of this.

A photo of black sand forming. (Credit: Philip Maise; Wikimedia Commons)

These very volcanoes are also responsible for creating some of the most beautiful rainforests to be found anywhere in the world, as well as wetlands that provide homes for thousands of species, including endangered birds. Volcanic deposits are incredibly fertile and are overloaded with nutrients that plants thrive in, specifically magnesium, iron, and potassium. This makes Hawaii naturally fertile.

Although this is a very brief look at how Hawaii was formed, you have a clearer idea of what ancient Hawaii was like before any person had seen it. It was a fertile paradise just waiting to be discovered. And this ever-expanding chain of islands would soon become home to a whole new realm of life.

This process took millions of years, but we are going to fast forward through time to take a look at Polynesia.

An Introduction to Polynesia

Polynesia is a large group of islands in the Pacific Ocean. These islands were settled by Austronesian people, who we think came from Taiwan. So, when you hear the word Polynesians today, you should know that there are many people groups that make it up. Since they are closely related and can trace their roots to the same place, they are bunched together under this one umbrella term. For instance, Polynesians include the Māori people of New Zealand, Tahitians, Samoans, and even Hawaiians.

Some might argue that Hawaii is not technically a part of Polynesia proper, although it was certainly settled by the Polynesians, which means they would fall under that grouping regardless. In the past, Hawaii was considered to be a part of the South Sea Islands. Today, most believe that Hawaii is a part of Polynesia since it falls into the Polynesian Triangle.

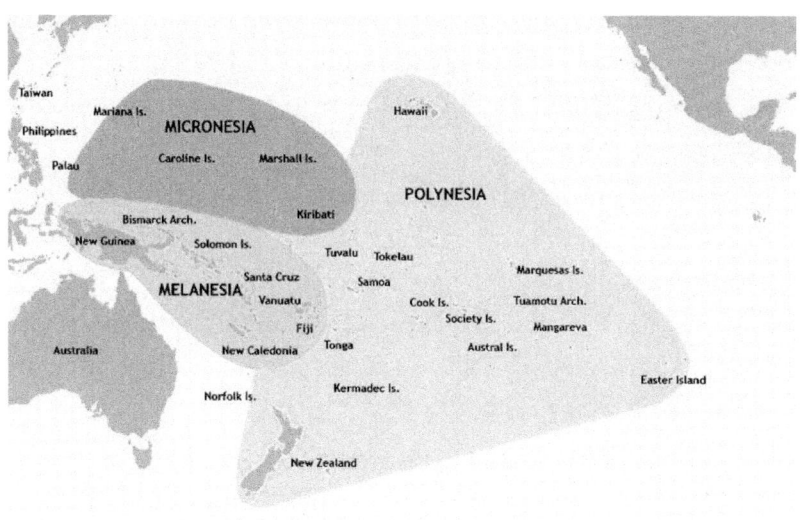

A map of the three major zones of Oceania. Note how Polynesia is shaped like a triangle. (Credit: Kahuroa; Wikimedia Commons)

Since the Polynesians spread from Southeast Asia into the Pacific, there is no central location for Polynesian history. The Austronesians began moving from Taiwan in 3000 BCE, but they only reached Polynesia around 900 BCE. They initially settled in Tonga and Samoa, and they would not explore more of Polynesia for nearly a thousand years. During that time, a cultural divide occurred between the people on the islands of Tonga and Samoa and those who lived in Fiji.

Although there were differences between the various Polynesian cultures, there were many similarities. For instance, their languages are related to each other. Today, there are thirty-eight Polynesian languages. They also share similar cultural traditions. The majority of them believed in polytheism and animism. Animism is the belief that deities or other supernatural powers lived within nature, such as animals, plants, and even handmade objects.

Expressing Through Art

It is important to note that the dates that have been mentioned are rough estimates since there was no writing system at the time. However, whereas writing how we know it today did not exist, the Polynesians are famed for using tattoos to record information and messages.

Polynesian tattoo art remains incredibly distinctive today. Back then (and in some cases today, especially when it comes to traditional tattooing), it contained a lot of information. Tattoos were used for a variety of purposes, such as telling important events of their life, expressing their status in society, honoring their ancestors, or safeguarding their health.

Polynesian tattoos usually consisted of curved lines, crosses, and circles. They were found on faces, hands, arms, legs, torsos, and other places on the body.

Although many Polynesian cultures use tattooing, we are going to focus on the Native Hawaiians here. They called the practice *kākau*. It was a very complicated process, and only experts (kahunas) could do it. It was a spiritual experience for everyone involved. According to a modern-day master of Hawaiian tattooing, Keli'i, one has to learn how to use their left hand to tattoo since this was the hand that channeled "spiritual intent."

The process is also incredibly painful. The pigment would be applied to the skin via a needle made from bone. This would be tied to a stick and then struck with a mallet. Essentially, the kahunas would tap the designs on the body. Typically, someone else would need to be there to help stretch the skin. These sessions would last three to five hours, and depending on the design, one might need to have multiple sessions. And if one could not endure the pain, they would leave with an incomplete tattoo. Everyone would know that person was cowardly with just one quick glance.

Some of the most popular designs were lizards, crescent fans, woven reeds, and other intricate patterns. Women could also get tattoos, although these were usually on their hands and wrists.

It should be emphasized that there were differences in both tattoos and the tattooing process among the Polynesian cultures. However, there would be some similarities, such as the fish hook design. If you were to travel to a new island and meet a new culture, you could usually tell who the leaders were, what someone's role was, and what kind of experiences they had, all thanks to their tattoos.

Chapter 2 – Arrival of the Polynesians

When it comes to any kind of ancient history, it is always a challenge to know where to begin, but interestingly with Hawaii, it is rather simple.

Our journey starts back in the year 400 CE. Most historians agree that the history of Hawaii started around this year, although the habitation of the islands was a process that occurred over a few hundred years.

Hawaii Finds Its People

The Polynesians were incredible seamen and navigators. They could sail without instruments by reading the stars. But even without modern-day technology, they were able to find their way across thousands of miles of open ocean. Sometimes they explored the ocean for fun. Sometimes it was because they needed to expand. The Polynesians also went on long voyages to trade with other islands or tribes. And when they traveled, they brought chickens, pigs, dogs, noni fruit, and kava with them.

There is no doubt that the Polynesians were successful in what they did. Their island hopping was very much fueled by their knowledge about currents in open water, which allowed them to plan their course, calculate when the best time to leave for specific islands would be, and when to return home. They knew when certain winds would be favorable for their journey.

It is this skill that allowed them to reach Hawaii in the first place. But before they reached Hawaii, they made settlements along the way. The Polynesians might have felt the need to create new settlements due to overpopulation. If there were too many people on their home island, the resources would become too stretched. In addition, the Polynesian tribes were known to engage in conflict, both internally with one another and on an island-to-island basis. There is evidence that suggests less impactful tribes, either due to numbers, resources, or strategies, could have fled these conflicts and surrendered their territories in the process, thus taking to the oceans to hunt for new lands.

Some of these settlements were made on the Marquesas Islands. These islands are about 2,336 miles from Hawaii and less than 1,000 miles from Tahiti.

The Polynesians first came across these lands around 100 to 700 CE, although some contend that they arrived much earlier, perhaps as early as 340 BCE. It was the paradise they had hoped for. Although most islands in the Pacific are fairly fertile, the Marquesas Islands were not. They were actually dry. This is because the islands are the first break for easterly winds, which causes droughts on the island.

Due to these droughts, there was a lack of vegetation and freshwater sources on the island, which caused massive problems for the settlers. Fortunately, due to their skills of being able to survive at sea for long periods of time, they could hang make a living, but it was certainly a struggle.

Historians believe the Polynesians who settled on the Marquesas Islands used them as a base while they explored the surrounding areas. They had much better prospects in other places, which is why the Marquesan lifestyle evolved much differently compared to that, for example, in Tahiti.

The lack of hygiene and malnutrition were issues that needed to be solved because they led to frequent miscarriages, which eventually made it impossible for the population to maintain itself at a stable level. It is believed that the Polynesians left the Marquesas Islands to find a place that was better suited for farming.

Historians today believe that the Polynesians sailed from the Marquesas Islands to the Hawaiian Islands around 400 CE. Some place the discovery of the islands to 300 CE, while others place it as late as 600 CE. This book will be using the general consensus of 400 CE. The reason scholars have a hard time pinpointing the exact date is due to the lack of a writing system. Although tattoos could record important events, these events would not come with dates. And stories that were passed down from generation to generation would not include precise years either.

How It Was All Made Possible

As stated above, the Polynesians were known for their skilled mariners and sailors, and their entire history is full of their feats of exploration and settling in foreign lands. So, it is not surprising that they were able to reach an archipelago as remote as Hawaii.

Polynesian canoes relied on the power of sails and paddles. They would use outrigger canoes, which could be simple dugout canoes or larger vessels. Typically, three or four boats would travel the oceans together to ensure mutual success. During the nights, they could stay in touch by blowing through a conch shell. It is clear just how advanced the Polynesians were, and it is easy to see why they were able to thrive.

Take a moment to imagine what this would have been like. You would have been setting out from a tropical island that contained everything you had ever known, setting out into the waters that had kept you safe. What new opportunities were out there waiting? And what dangers lurked on the horizon?

The Magic of Polynesian Sailing

The Polynesians' sailing and navigation skills were truly astounding, especially when you consider how far they had to travel. It is certainly a worthwhile tangent to dive into.

A drawing of a small Polynesian sailing boat. Smaller vessels like this would typically be used for traveling between islands. Larger two-sailed boats were typically used for longer voyages. These larger vessels were capable of holding up to thirty to fifty people. (Credit: Wikimedia Commons)

Evidence shows that the Polynesians were capable of reaching nearly every single island that can be found within the Polynesian Triangle; its three points are Hawaii, Easter Island, and New Zealand. This is why there are so many similarities in the cultures within this area.

But how did they do it?

Well, there is no single right answer since the Polynesians employed a variety of techniques. They studied the stars and followed the flight paths of birds. Simply put, the Polynesians were masters of their craft. Since there was no writing or recording, all of these skills were passed down through verbal communication and experience.

Navigating the Stars

By far the most impressive way the Polynesians navigated was by tracking the locations of the stars in the sky, a technique that was optimized and perfected over thousands of years. Stars hold their celestial position all year round, but they rise at different times depending on the seasons. This means that every single star in the sky has a particular declination.

When you track this movement, whether it is a star rising or setting, you begin to track your geographic location in relation to certain stars. To many readers living in the modern age, passing down knowledge like this without being able to write it down might seem incredible. But to the Polynesians, it was second nature.

The Polynesians would set off into the waters and head toward a star that sat near the horizon. Once their chosen star rose too high, they would switch to a lower one. It was almost like solving a dot-to-dot puzzle in the sky, as there was a route of stars you had to follow if you wanted to travel to a certain place.

Equally as incredible, the Polynesians would also measure the elevation of stars, which allowed them to determine their own latitude. Therefore, they were able to locate and navigate themselves to islands that they already knew the locations of. If you wanted to travel to an island, you would basically sail along with the latitude measurement until you got there, using the star routes to help you navigate.

If you couple this with the rest of the techniques the Polynesians used, you can understand how the Polynesians did what seems impossible. With these navigational tools at hand, they would have had a relatively solid format for finding their way around the ocean.

The Swells of the Ocean

Another essential navigational trick the Polynesians had up their sleeves was identifying and tracking the swells of the oceans. These are waves not caused by nearby winds; rather, they are the result of wind from distant low-pressure systems.

There is an endless number of habitable islands within the Polynesian Triangle, and there are chains of islands that are thousands of miles long. This means that the ocean currents are fairly easy to predict along an island chain.

Say you were a Polynesian trying to travel to an island. You could travel to a few islands you knew and meet up with other tribes and communities who lived there. You could ask them about the swells and currents in that local area, which would help you get to the next island. And from there, the process would continue until you found the place you wanted.

Even if you found yourself in an unfamiliar area, you could simply identify the swells and currents you had experienced before. Since you would be in the same part of the world, they would be fairly similar. When you factor in wind directions and star navigation, you can see how the Polynesians were able to become fairly accurate in finding their way around and being able to discover new places.

Following the Birds

The most powerful navigational method the Polynesians had was watching the flight patterns of birds. The Pacific Ocean is home to many bird migration routes, and the Polynesians would have naturally become familiar with them. Understanding and noting the patterns of these birds was, therefore, a great way of figuring out where you were and where you were going.

The Polynesians used different types of birds to navigate the Pacific. Some of these birds include the white tern, Pacific long-tailed cuckoo, Pacific golden plover, noddy tern, and the bristle-thighed curlew.

Navigators would follow the migrations of these birds. For example, it was known that the white tern would fly out from its island home to hunt for food early in the mornings in the open ocean and then go back to land at night. If you set sail in the morning and were looking to find land, you could just sail in the reverse direction from where the white birds were flying.

Of course, nesting seasons would alter this pattern slightly, but that was all knowledge that the Polynesians built up over the years and could use to their advantage. This way of navigating was so successful that it was taught to US soldiers during World War II as a way of finding land if they found themselves on a shipwrecked boat or lost in the air.

What is more, it is believed that many Polynesians would take a shore-sighted bird with them on their boats. These were birds who supposedly refused to land on the water. For instance, the frigatebird would not land in water since their feathers would get too wet to fly. If navigators thought they were getting close to shore, they would release the frigatebird. If the sailors were not close to land, the bird would just fly back to the boat. However, if they were close to land, the bird would fly to the shore, and the Polynesians would follow it.

This was just one of the skills that set the Polynesians up for success and allowed them to span all over this area of the world. Naturally, for exploration and discovery, as well as for reasons like warfare and a lack of resources, the Polynesians set out to find what new places they could find.

Discovering a New Home

And so, with all this information on how the Polynesians lived and navigated the seas, it comes as no surprise that they were able to make it to the island of Hawaii after migrating over the centuries across the Pacific Ocean.

And during these centuries, the Polynesian explorers were able to collect a vast number of resources to help them with their efforts, such as a variety of plants. They also had seeds for banana plants, breadfruit, and taro, just to name a few plants they ate. In addition, they brought along livestock, such as pigs, dogs, and chickens. Some of these were brought from their initial home, but they collected some of these as they hopped from island to island in search of a new home.

And eventually, they found that home in the Hawaiian Islands.

The first settlers of Hawaii landed in Ka Lae, which is the southernmost tip of what is today known as the main island of Hawai'i. This is the largest and most southerly island in the archipelago.

It was during this time that Hawai'i was given its name. Hawai'i comes from the Polynesian word *Hawaiki* (the w is pronounced as a v), which means "homeland." The preferred pronunciation of Hawai'i today is "huh-wah-ee" or "huh-vai-ee." There is discussion over whether Hawaii should be pronounced with a "w" or a "v," with most Native Hawaiians tending to use the "v" pronunciation. On top of this, the glottal stop is often ignored by tourists. The glottal stop is similar to the pause in "uh-oh." Chances are that no one will look at you twice if you pronounce it without the glottal stop, though.

Some Native Hawaiians contend that people had been living on the islands by the time the Polynesians arrived. They were pushed inland when the Polynesians arrived. The people who support this theory point to Hawaiian mythology, which mentions the Menehune, a race of dwarfs. They built temples and fish ponds, which were both things the arriving Polynesians continued to build. However, it seems more likely that the Polynesians were the first settlers of the islands.

The Polynesians had a few difficult first years, but eventually, they settled and survived long enough to see their land prosper into something beautiful. Since they were highly skilled farmers and fishermen, they were able to thrive.

Due to how successful the Polynesians were, it was not long before they spread out and populated the other major Hawaiian Islands. Now, remember this was all happening around 400 to 1000 CE. This means it is hard to know exactly what kind of lifestyle the people had in terms of what their customs were and how they actually lived on a day-to-day basis. After all, the Polynesians did not write down what occurred to them, and the artifacts we have access to are limited in what they tell us.

However, based on the evidence that has been uncovered, we know that the Polynesians were the sole inhabitants of the Hawaiian Islands for nearly six hundred years. Around 1000 CE (although some place this date earlier), the Tahitians arrived and discovered this tropical wonderland for themselves, thus joining the existing population.

The Hawaiian civilization was born.

Chapter 3 – The World of Pre-Contact Hawaii

Between the years of 1000 and 1778 CE, Hawaii was pretty much untouched and relatively unknown by most of the world. This is the period we label as ancient Hawaii. This was a time when the tribes and communities lived off the land. Although they had their own issues, as every civilization does, the issues Native Hawaiians had to face tended to be a little different than the seemingly progressive and often turbulent ones that affected other populations around the world.

In 1778, explorer Captain James Cook would arrive on the islands and began the process of connecting the archipelago with the rest of the world. But what were the islands like for those nearly eight hundred years?

After the islands were discovered, the Polynesians inhabited them. It has been suggested that they arrived in two waves. The first came from the Marquesas Islands in the south around 400 CE, whereas the second wave came from Tahiti, likely around the 9th or 10th century. Over the years, these populations grew, with the islands of Hawaii accommodating an incredible 300,000 people before the arrival of Cook himself. (It should be noted that the actual number of Hawaiian residents is unknown. The conservative estimates go as low as 100,000, while the higher estimates go to nearly a million.)

Ancient Hawaiians were lightly brown-skinned people, and they typically had black hair that was either straight or wavy. These people were also on the larger side, similar to the Māori people from New Zealand. The ancient Hawaiians were broad and tall but also athletic, lean, and muscular.

Most of the cultural traits that these societies followed were similar to other Polynesian tribes and cultures at the time. For example, a ruling class or a ruling royal family led the tribes and made the decisions. The supreme ruler of each generation was known as the *aliʻi nui*. The word *aliʻi* (the noble class) is a familiar word in other Polynesian languages, but in the Māori language, this concept would be known as *ariki*.

These ruling classes typically engaged in inbreeding to keep the bloodline pure. Many of the male leaders, who were known as chiefs, would practice polygyny, which means they had more than one wife. As we will explore later, most of the kings in the monarchy had multiple wives. One ruler might have had as many as thirty wives!

How the Society Viewed Land

Since this was an island society, there is no doubt that land was one of the most important and valuable commodities in Hawaii. It was the main contributing factor when it came to distinguishing wealth amongst the people, much as it is today. Land ownership defined boundaries and detailed how authority and leadership would be doled out.

For a clear idea of how this worked, you would have to take the whole of Hawaii and divide it up into "sections of pie," as many sources describe it.

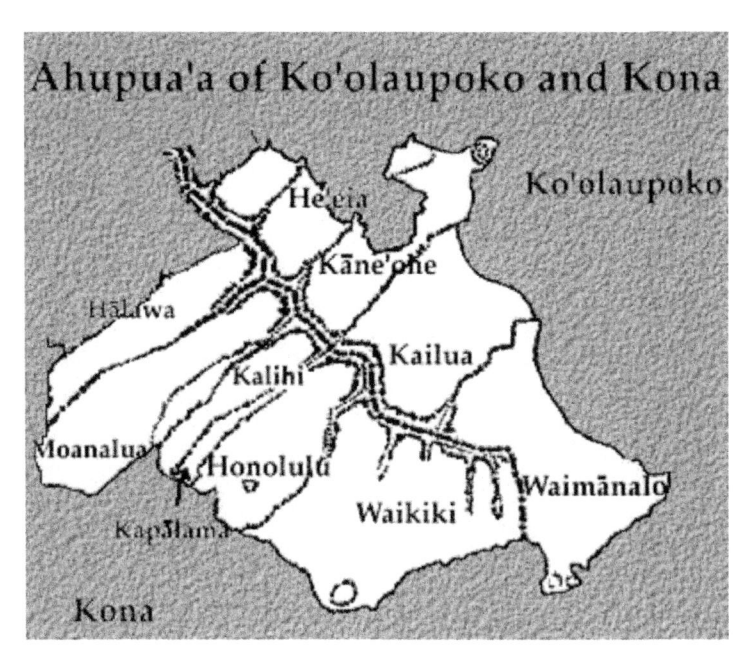

The "sections of pie" would ultimately look a little something like this.

These land divisions were known as *moku*, with the island itself being called *mokupuni*. Each *moku* went from the very tip of the mountaintops to the shorelines of the ocean. The *moku* would be further divided into *ahupua'a*, and these would be divided into even smaller sections called *'ili*.

This system of division was what made the Hawaiian societies successful. They were self-contained, but they were also sustainable. The people were capable of living amongst themselves and working alongside communities in neighboring divisions.

Those who lived in the mountains specialized in growing food on nutritious and fertilized land while making tools and using the forests for resources.

Volcanic activity is one of the reasons that Hawaii is known as an epicenter of biodiversity. Recent research has found that volcanic eruptions actually create a type of soil that is incredibly favorable for plant life.

According to a study published recently in *Science*, lava from the Kīlauea and Mauna Loa volcanoes has played a key role in the development of the island of Hawai'i's rich coastal ecosystems. Over time, as lava flows into the ocean, it cools and breaks down into various minerals, such as calcium, iron, potassium, and phosphorus, which are necessary for plant life to thrive. These minerals mix with organic debris and bacteria and become a "volcanic smorgasbord" for the native plants and animals of Hawai'i, although this phenomenon affected the other islands as well.

As lava cools and interacts with seawater, it also forms clay that is resistant to heat, allowing for plant life to continue growing even after the eruptions cease. This consistent source of fresh nutrients allows land that would otherwise be desert and infertile to be teeming with life.

"The whole chemistry of the soils changes when you have lava flowing over them," said the study's co-author Dave Karl, a geochemist at the University of Hawaii's School of Ocean and Earth Science Technology. "It has an immediate effect that declines over time, but the lasting legacy of lava flowing over the landscape is that it creates extremely good growing conditions."

While the ancient Hawaiians would not have known the science behind this, they would have indeed reaped the benefits. Thus, they were able to create a thriving society with plenty of resources to go around.

And the way the islands ran was fairly well-organized. Those who worked on the land and up in the mountains traded with those who lived on the coastlines. Of course, people who called the coastlines home were experts at fishing and rearing animals. This knowledge would be passed down through the generations from their ancestors, who we, of course, know to be masters of the sea. This partnership ensured that every islander had access to things they wanted or needed.

It is important to note that these earlier divisions still impact Hawaiian society today. Many of the *ahupua'a* are officially recognized by law today, with the most notable being the regions of Waikiki, Nanakuli, Kailua, and Honolulu.

The word *ahupua'a* is formed from two words: *ahu* and *pua'a*. *Ahu* refers to the stacks of rocks and stones that were laid out at the edges of each district boundary. The word *ahu* literally means stone altar or mound.

These stacks were typically laid out to represent an image of a pig or *pua'a*. Usually, these were carved wooden images of a pig's head. Moreover, pigs were laid on altars as offerings to other tribe leaders as signs of peace and respect. However, other offerings were sometimes used instead.

While the *ali'i nui* ran each island and acted as the ruling king, they would have help in doing so. Each district (*moku*) would have a chief called an *ali'i 'aimoku*. Each division of the *moku* (*ahupua'a*) would have a *konohiki*. These were lesser chiefs, and they would ensure that the proper tribute was paid to the king. They also attended to the people's needs, such as making sure there was enough water to go around and distributing land.

The organization of the islands was quite astounding, even by today's standards. While the infrastructure was not advanced, especially compared to other civilizations that existed around or before this time, such as the Roman or Chinese empires, there is no doubt that the Hawaiians were thriving.

The Essence of Taro and Other Foods

While Hawaii was divided so the people could better control it, most Hawaiian divisions had pretty much everything they needed to succeed and thrive. The ocean was used for fishing, and the trees and jungles were full of foods like coconuts. Taro was one of the most popular food sources. In addition to being the primary food source of the island, it also held sacred properties. It is still incredibly popular today, especially throughout the Asian and Polynesian territories.

Taro comes from the Araceae plant family, and it was widely used throughout ancient Hawaiian culture as food and for its proclaimed healing and medicinal properties. And the ancient Hawaiians were actually onto something there. Nowadays, modern science has proven that taro is full of potassium and vitamins, including the essential vitamins A, B, C, and E. It is also rich in copper and magnesium, making it a great all-around foodstuff. Perhaps this is why it is still so popular today.

In fact, ancient Hawaiians revered taro so much that it is even included as a part of their origin story.

Long ago, in the days when Hawaii was young, the Hawaiian people used to tell stories about how their islands were formed. Many of these legends have been passed down through the generations by word of mouth, yet others are preserved in ancient chants and writings. Some claim that the gods still live in Hawai'i today, watching over her people and protecting them from harm.

In the beginning, everything in the Hawaiian Islands was made by the gods, from volcanic fire to misty rain and from palm trees and lush green forests to jagged cliffs and golden beaches. The drinking water that flows from deep within the earth's crust to mana—a spiritual energy that permeates all living things—is all due to the gods.

There are many different legends, but the one we will retell here involves the sky god, Wākea. He married Papahānaumoku, a princess and a goddess of the earth. They created the islands together. They also created a daughter, whom they named Ho'ohokukalani. She grew up to be incredibly beautiful and became the keeper of the stars.

Her father longed to have her. But Wākea knew it would be impossible to bed Ho'ohokukalani while Papahānaumoku was around, so he sent her away. He ended up sleeping with his daughter, and she bore a child. Unfortunately, the child was stillborn, and the heartbroken parents buried the child on Earth, where Hawaii was. A taro plant grew where the body had been laid to rest.

A second child was eventually born to the two gods: Haloa. This child became the father of the Hawaiian people. He knew the taro plant had come from his older brother, so he thought the taro plant contained his spirit and essence. The ancient Hawaiians held the same kind of respect for the taro plant. It was a love that has been passed down through the many generations of Hawaiians who lived on the islands. Even today, it is seen as a sacred plant.

Therefore, there were strict rules in place when it came to taro plants. They were so strict, in fact, that only men were allowed to prepare any dish that used taro. As a note, for those interested in trying taro themselves, you must make sure to cook it. Almost every part of the taro plant is toxic in its raw form.

From an ecological standpoint, Hawaii is the perfect place for such a plant to grow. The two most important things that taro needs to grow are warm weather and moisture. Hawaii is surrounded by the ocean, but it is home to numerous water reservoirs and a handful of lakes.

Taro was often grown in two ways on the island. The first method involved creating a pond. Taro would be cultivated near this pond, and they would later flood the land. When it came to growing taro on the mountains, where the land was very fertile, farmers would dig holes almost a foot deep and plant the taro there. Once they began to sprout, the farmers would cover the holes with mud.

What is more, the raised ground of the mountains causes rain clouds coming in off the ocean to cluster and condensate, thus creating opportunities for the land to flood. This would send essential minerals and nutrients from the mountaintops down to the growing lands. In short, crops had ample opportunities to thrive on the islands.

These flooded, wet areas or irrigation fields were known as *lo'i*, and they were known for being constantly submerged under several inches of water at all times. There is even clear evidence that many of the islands were covered in conduits that traveled from the flooded taro fields. They would carry water to more remote parts of the island and society in general.

This created the perfect environment to grow many crops. Thus, the valley areas where this farming took place, such as the Hanalei Valley on the island of Kaua'i, were home to many people.

Some of the other foods the Hawaiians were famous for growing included staples like breadfruit, sweet potatoes, sugarcane, and bananas.

Even outside the farmlands, the rest of the land was resourcefully used. For instance, wood from nearby forests was used for constructing buildings and tools and for fueling fires.

Down at the coast, you would find people fishing or searching for other marine life. Women and children would take part in inland fishing, which saw the Native Hawaiians exploring shallow reef areas and pools for aquatic life. These could be caught by hand, although nets, baskets, and spears could also be used. The Hawaiians used plants to their advantage, creating concoctions that would stun the fish and draw them to the surface.

A photograph of a Hawaiian fisherman, 1915. (Credit: Historic Photographs of Old Hawai'i)

Canoe fishing tended to be reserved for men only. Fishermen would paddle out to deep-sea fishing areas, with knowledge of the best areas being passed down through the generations. The fishermen could either catch fish in the open sea or use the stone-walled fishing circles, which encased the fish, making them easier to catch. Some of these stone circles still stand to this day and date back over one thousand years.

Fish were often eaten right then and there, but the Hawaiians did preserve fish by drying them. Sometimes, they would salt them before laying them on racks on the beach so they could dry in the sun. Some of the most popular marine life captured besides fish include crabs, octopi, lobsters, eels, seaweed, and shrimp.

In short, the Hawaiians were incredibly successful in their efforts to feed their families and create a permanent home.

The Craftsmanship of Ancient Hawaii

There is no doubt the ancient Hawaiians were successful, for the most part, in what they set out to achieve. They were farmers, navigators, explorers, and fishermen at heart. Some consider them to be the best who ever lived.

But while the Native Hawaiians tend to be remembered for their adventurous nature, they were also innovative craftsmen. The ancient Hawaiians did not have metal pots or tools at the time. Even though the Bronze and Iron Ages had come and gone, Hawaii was far from this kind of innovation due to the isolated nature of the islands. On top of this, these kinds of metals were not even present on the islands, so there was not much chance of making items out of them. They likely had knowledge of metals, but this was due to debris washing onshore.

Instead, the people used more traditional materials for their tools. Some of the most common resources were shells, bones, stones, and even the teeth of both humans and animals.

However, the artistry and passion that Native Hawaiians had with their work are beyond comparison. The Romans were known for their infrastructure and architecture, while the Hawaiians were (and still are) renowned for their expert craftsmanship.

Back then, houses in Hawaii were built with carved wooden frames and thatched with strung leaves. Sure, this was not the Colosseum, but the homes were perfect for the tropical conditions that the Hawaiians lived in. Evidence suggests that public buildings were built in a similar way, and they were even kitted out with benches and tables to sit at.

Life was simple. Much of the food was cooked using hot stones that were heated via campfires. The food was then left to simmer on top of holes dug into the ground. However, the vast majority of food, including fish, was eaten raw.

In terms of clothing, the traditional image you might have of Hawaiians is what was true at the time, which is likely where many of the stereotypes stem from. Men would wear a traditional loincloth, known as a *malo*. Women would wear skirts called *pa'u*. These were not grass skirts, which is perhaps the common image of Hawaiian women's clothing. These would only be introduced to the islands in the late 1800s.

Rather, both *malo* and *pa'u* were made of plant fibers. Tops were occasionally worn as well, but since the climate was so hot, many went without. This would change once the Europeans arrived, as did many other things. So, yes, the idea that Hawaiian women and other women of the Pacific wore coconut bras is entirely incorrect.

Much of their clothing was made from *kapa*, which is barkcloth. On other Pacific islands, this was called *tapa*. *Kapa* would be made from pounding the bark of certain trees, which would turn the bark into fabric.

The bark would be stripped from the tree, with the most common tree in Hawaii used to make *kapa* being the wauke or paper mulberry tree. The bark would be cleaned, boiled or steamed, and then beaten. And it was *really* beaten. While the bark was being pounded, the fibers of the bark would stretch, causing the material to soften. After this, it would be dried in the sun to make it strong.

The people would then dye the material and create intricate patterns on them. This cloth was used for clothing, as well as blankets and other decorative items, like tapestries or bedding. Today, Hawaiians do not typically wear *kapa*, as it is an incredibly time-consuming process, but it is sometimes worn on important occasions, like weddings. Hawaiians are working on preserving this beautiful art form, so it will hopefully be around for a very long time.

An example of tapa from Samoa, 1890s. Keep in mind this was done entirely by hand. (Credit: Wikimedia Commons)

Of course, we cannot talk about Hawaiian craftsmanship without mentioning their skillful boatbuilding, especially since sailing and exploring were what they were best known for. The ancient Hawaiians mainly stuck with canoes, which they often used to travel to fish with or between the various islands.

Their canoes were about the same size as recreational canoes today, between fifteen to twenty-four feet long. However, their canoes varied in size. Double-hulled canoes would be as long as thirty to seventy feet long. The largest one ever measured by a European explorer was around 107 feet long! These large canoes were necessary for carrying not just human passengers but also livestock and other forms of cargo, such as crops.

Ancient Hawaiians made their boats out of trees. But it was not as easy as finding a tree and deciding it would make a great canoe. A person would have to consult a kahuna (an expert) who specialized in canoe-building. He would have to decipher his dreams and figure out which tree to cut down.

Canoes were typically made from koa trees, which are very plentiful on the Hawaiian Islands even today. Prayers would be invoked, and rituals would be performed before, during, and after the tree was cut down. After this, the boat would be shaped using various tools.

The Hawaiians used a number of different tools to make their canoes. The stone adze was probably the most important tool of them all, as it was used in the felling process and the carving process. It was a tool you could find in most households. Adzes were made from basalt, which is a hard, black volcanic rock. They would be tied to a handle with cords made from coconut fiber. These cords played an important role in the canoe-building process as well. The islanders would use ropes or cords made from coconut fiber to lash together the logs and rig up the sails.

Different parts of the boat would be crafted out of other trees. For instance, the boom, the part of the boat that allows you to adjust the angle of the sail, would be made out of lighter wood. For instance, it could be made from a tree called wiliwili. Not all canoes had sails; some just had paddles, while others used both.

The Gender Differences in Ancient Hawaii

We have touched on this a little already, such as how men were able to have multiple wives and how women were not allowed to handle sacred foods like taro. Now we will dive into some of the other gender norms of the time so we can have a clearer understanding of what life was like back then.

While there were rules in place that stated how women should act and what they could and could not do, many believed that women were still respected and treated well in their communities, especially in comparison to how other women were treated at the time. However, this is, of course, both subjective and relative.

When the missionaries arrived on the islands in 1820, they described Hawaiian women as "lazy." Men were responsible for carrying out any hard labor tasks that needed to be done, as well as all of the fishing and agricultural work. Men were also in charge of most of the cooking.

On the other hand, women were in charge of making the clothing, crafting mats, and creating any fabric products that needed to be made. They were also responsible, for the most part, for raising children, and they would also collect shellfish and do other light labor tasks.

Nevertheless, just like the men, women would enjoy ample downtime to participate in many activities, including swimming, dancing, surfing, racing, and playing games, which included variations on checkers (*kōnane*) and bowling (*maika*). Gambling on the outcome of these games was very popular.

Interestingly, ancient Hawaiians had a third gender role, which was known as *māhū*. This *māhū* gender (meaning "in the middle") is known in both Hawaiian and other Tahitian cultures. It is usually adopted by those in religious or spiritual roles. Typically, a *māhū* was born male but would become gender-neutral once they progressed into their cultural role.

Since temples were off-limits to women, the *māhū* performed the hula dances to the goddesses and performed the feminine roles in these spaces. The *māhū* were important in Hawaiian culture, and they were even responsible for naming the newborn children. Today, *māhū* is used to refer to different genders and sexual orientations.

Wāhine is the term used in Hawaii for women. Men would be called *kāne*. Today, when people think of Hawaiian women and their role in culture, hula usually pops into their minds first. There are different forms of hula, but the traditional style of the dance celebrates chiefs and deities. Every motion of the dance signifies something. For example, hand movements could represent the ocean's waves. These dances were seen as holy, so practicing this dance was deemed essential. A chant would often be said during the dance, and the common instruments used during these ceremonies included gourd drums and gourd rattles. As an interesting side note, these chants would contain important historical information, which was one way Hawaiian history was passed down.

However, no one is quite sure where the dance originated. According to tradition, it was a gift from the gods. On top of this, it is not known for sure if women were allowed to dance the hula initially. When James Cook arrived in 1778, he noted that he saw women dancing. It does seem likely that women did perform this dance, as its origins tend to note that the early dancers of hula were goddesses. Although we cannot put complete faith in legends and myths, there is typically a kernel of truth. If goddesses were seen as the original hula dancers, it only stands to reason that women could also dance it. Today, hula is typically danced by women.

In ancient Hawaii, women hula dancers would have worn just a skirt and no top. Ancient Hawaii had a different view of sex and nudity than other places did at this time. The Hawaiians did not see their genitals as a shameful thing. The only reason they covered the lower half of their body was to protect it. In fact, nudity was seen as a sign of respect. Of course, that depended on the situation. Being nude might also show submission or acted as a way to ask for forgiveness.

At a young age, both boys and girls would be taught what to expect from sex and their roles for the future. Hawaiian society did not place shame on the act of sex, and the adults encouraged adolescents to experiment. However, the act of an older man sleeping with a younger boy was not the norm as it was in places like ancient Greece. And when it came to the act of sex itself, age did not play as big of a role as it did in Europe, for example. Rather, it was based on maturity. Ancient Hawaiians' views on sex were incredibly progressive, perhaps even more so than in most contemporary societies. Of course, along with a lot of other things, these views changed once the Europeans arrived.

But there were still boundaries and rules in place that needed to be followed. When it came to female *aliʻi*, especially the first-born daughter, virginity was important. They would be betrothed at a very young age so they knew what was expected of them. Once they were married to a chief, they could have multiple lovers. In addition, when any woman experienced her monthly cycle, known as *waimaka lehua*, they had to live entirely separately from the men until it was over. This was a common practice in many cultures, and it is still practiced today in some places today.

There were also other rules. For example, men and women were not allowed to eat together, and their meals could not be prepped together. An *imu*, which was basically a firepit oven, was used for prepping the men's food, while a different one was used for the women's food. Men and women were not even allowed to eat together. Instead, they would eat in separate huts, which were known as *hale mua* (men's eating hut) and *hale ʻaina* (women's eating hut). *Nā hale* ("the houses") were the buildings that made up the community; they were built using logs, thatched grasses, and small stones.

Even the foods that men and women could eat differed. In addition to being restricted from consuming taro, women were not allowed to eat other sacred foods, including coconuts, pigs, certain kinds of fish, and bananas.

Every one of these rules was defined by the *kapu*, or the law of Hawaii, which is something we will go into detail later. However, it is important to keep this in mind, for these rules were not just suggestions. Failing to abide by them or breaking the *kapu* in any way was punishable by death.

However (and this is a big however), how men and women were treated dramatically varied from island to island, and many had their own differences when it came to the *kapu*. For example, on Maui and Hawai'i (the Big Island), common women were allowed to till the ground and collect both food and firewood. On Ni'ihau, women were allowed to fish and could even be priests. On other islands, these roles were strictly prohibited.

All that being said, Hawaii celebrated women. The ancient Hawaiians had a chant of creation known as the *Kumulipo*. The verses describe the first human being, which was a woman known as La'ila'i. Another legend, which we recounted above, states that Haloa was the first human. Hawaiian legends do have some differences, something that is common with most ancient civilizations. Regardless, women were seen as life-givers, and their importance in ancient Hawaiian society is clear.

The Caste System

Ancient Hawaii had a social structure similar to a caste system. The ranks were as follows:

- Royalty, chiefs, and royal advisors; they were known as *ali'i*.
- Priests and skilled professionals; they were known as a *kahuna*.
- Common people; they were known as *maka'ainana*.
- Prisoners of war and slaves; they were known as *kauwā*.

Within the kahuna class were skilled craftsmen, doctors, and dancers. The *maka'ainana* class consisted of all the traditional worker roles, including farmers, fishermen, and simpler craftsmen. We will touch on this later, but an individual's rank was defined by bloodlines and how much mana that individual had. Mana basically refers to one's inner spiritual power. You could also call this some kind of divine power. It was possible for a person to rise through the ranks as long as there was proof of the required mana level.

The *kauwā* class was reserved for slaves, prisoners of war, and their descendants. People from this class would often be used in human sacrifices. Both animals and humans would be sacrificed at temples called *luakini heiau*. It is likely they were sacrificed to appease the gods or perhaps the chiefs. There is also the possibility that they were sacrificed to bring about good omens.

The Housing of Ancient Hawaii

Up until the 18th century, buildings that were used for housing were pretty much unchanged. However, as time passed, their methods became more refined. The buildings for the royalty became more elaborate, and the structures became sturdier. Design-wise, though, everything remained relatively the same.

Perhaps the earliest form of housing was what we would call simple shacks or shelters. More defined building designs would later be used for homes, with simpler ones being used by fishermen and for the storage of tools and equipment, such as farming tools and boats. They were also used to store foodstuffs and materials like fabrics.

However, the everyday buildings in Hawaii displayed a lot about the occupants inside. The patterns in which the roof was woven, the plant fibers that were used, and the type of wood that it was constructed out of could all define the person who owned the property. It could show off their caste, skill, wealth, and profession.

This way of defining a person was so popular that when James Cook arrived in 1778, he used this kind of symbolism to identify houses and buildings based on their religious value and classed the inhabitants accordingly.

For more regal individuals, such as the kings and chiefs, feathers were presented at the front of the properties. This royal standard was known as *kāhili*. This was a symbol that all the chiefs and upper families would use to display their status. It was, in essence, a long pole with a cluster of feathers on the end. *Kāhili* could only be carried by *ali'i*, and they would regularly be used in ceremonies and rituals.

The Vibrant Culture of Hawaii

While Hawaiians were undoubtedly skilled in the way they organized and lived their lives, it was not all work and no play. Hawaiians excelled in their athletic pursuits, so it makes sense that this was one of the most celebrated aspects of their culture. Athletic contests were held regularly to figure out who was the best man or woman of a tribe, but they were also used as a source of friendly competition and to bring neighboring tribes closer together.

There is evidence that shows Hawaiians participated in many sports, including wrestling, bowling, running, spear throwing, swimming, fighting (boxing), and even a native form of surfing.

Surfing is something that is commonly associated with Hawaii today, so it is worth exploring a little bit more. Surfing was not always done on surfboards. Ancient Hawaiians would bodysurf or even surf on their canoes. Some people claim that Hawaiians invented surfboarding, but that is likely not true, as this activity has been documented on many other islands in Polynesia. However, Hawaii probably had the most advanced form of it. The surfboard one used depended on one's class. The *ali'i* had slightly longer boards, which were made from lighter wood. Similar to canoe-building, crafting a surfboard involved intricate rituals. It was not as simple as cutting down a tree and fashioning it. These boards did not feature the iconic fin that surfboards have today; that would not be introduced until the 1930s. There were also rules when it came to catching waves. For instance, it went against the *kapu* for a commoner to ride a wave that an *ali'i* wanted to ride or was riding.

Another popular sport was lava sledding, which is called *he'e hōlua* in Hawaiian. They used a wooden sled called a *papa hōlua*. This sled would be around twelve feet long and six inches wide. Contrary to the name, actual lava was not involved. Rather, the courses were built along natural lava flow spots, which allowed the sled to reach maximum speeds. A person could stand, kneel, or lay down on the sled as they flew down the mountain. These sleds could go as fast as fifty miles per hour! Lava sledding was used as both a sport and for religious purposes.

An example of a papa hōlua. *(Credit: W. Nowicki; Wikimedia Commons)*

There is evidence that shows Hawaiians would gamble on many of these activities. While there was not any money passing hands on the islands, the Hawaiians would gamble with things like live pigs, coconuts, breadfruit, and bananas.

The Hawaiians enjoyed their downtime in other ways. The men and sometimes women would savor fermented drinks that could have narcotic effects. These were known as *awa* (pronounced "ah-vah"). Nowadays, this drink is known as kava. There was a special way to both create and drink *awa*, but it was not an addictive substance like alcohol.

Music was also an integral part of society. Hawaiians were fans of using instruments, such as nose flutes, string instruments, and even percussion drums. Their parties were both elaborate and engaging. Flowers were added to outfits in many different ways, especially during hula celebrations. This brings us to another popular image of Hawaii: leis. Leis are popular in most of Polynesia, but each culture used different flowers, leaves, seeds, and vines to create them. Leis would be worn or given to another person for many different reasons, such as a special occasion, but people could wear leis just because they wanted to. When it comes to Hawaii today, each island has its own lei, which is made with different flowers and represents different things.

On top of all this, the ancient Hawaiians loved poetry. Storytellers would bring to life the details of the Hawaiians' legendary, spiritual, and religious history. Evidence suggests that the most popular storytelling mediums were chanting, riddles, and sharing tribunal proverbs and teachings, which would have been passed down from generation to generation. Of course, Hawaiians did not have writing as we know it but instead used drawings and art, such as *kākau* (tattoo art). They would also draw on cave walls or create statues and small monuments.

Their primary way of communicating, though, was verbally and then passing that information along.

The Spiritual Beliefs of Ancient Hawaiians

Spiritual beliefs were a core part of Hawaiian culture. If animals appeared to individuals in a dream or vision, they were thought to be visits by family members who had passed away or their personal gods. They would carry messages or warnings to those who received them. Someone with more mana and, therefore, a deeper spiritual connection to the gods could have these visions for whole communities and tribes.

Religious practices were an important part of everyday life. For instance, prayers were considered to be vital. Prayers could be said at *heiaus*, which were the Hawaiians' name for their temples. As stated above, enclosed temples and religious spaces were off-limits for women. However, these sacred spaces were not open to the average man either. Only priests, chiefs, and kings could enter them during ancient times.

But not all *heiaus* were enclosed spaces. In fact, most of them were open-aired spaces. *Heiaus* would have different purposes; for instance, some were designated to help the sick while others were meant to encourage rain. Ancient Hawaiians would travel to these temples to pray for help with a particular concern or to thank the gods after being helped.

Most *heiaus* did not survive the test of time. It should be noted that this was not always due to the wear and tear of time; a good majority of them were torn down by Christian missionaries. Most of the ones that remained today were built later on, and some of them are closed to tourists due to their sacred nature.

Regardless, numerous temples were constructed and built across the islands, and they were regarded as special places of worship. Typically, these makeshift structures would have used materials like lava rock, thatched pili grass, and wood. Mini statues representing the gods would be made out of wood, and they would have been used as decorations and symbols that the people would then worship to prove their loyalty and dedication.

As with most ancient civilizations, Hawaii has tales that tell how the earth was created by the gods. The most popular legend tells of how Pele, the goddess of fire, and Nāmaka, the goddess of the sea, created the Hawaiian Islands. Whenever Pele was enraged, she would react by setting off volcanic eruptions around the archipelago. The magma would then flow down to the oceans, where it would fight with the water. Hence, Pele and Nāmaka were bitter rivals.

One of their fights got a little out of hand. Near Kauaʻi, Pele started fires, and Nāmaka responded by putting them out before fighting her sister. This is how the islands began to form.

The fight continued as the sisters headed southwest, with the fights creating the islands of Molokaʻi and Maui. The conflict even resulted in the formation of the Haleakalā volcano, a huge volcano that forms more than 75 percent of Maui. However, on Maui, Nāmaka was finally able to get the upper hand, and she killed Pele once and for all.

But Pele would not die so easily. Instead, she ended up traveling to the Big Island (Hawaiʻi), where she created Mauna Loa, one of the five volcanoes that make up the Big Island. Mauna Loa is one of the most active volcanoes on Earth today. This construction was so impressive and dominating that Nāmaka realized she would never be able to defeat Pele, and she conceded. Nowadays, the essence of Pele still resides in the peak of Halemaʻumaʻu, a volcanic crater that is a part of the Kīlauea volcano, while Nāmaka is confined to the ocean.

In addition to the gods told in this origin story, the Hawaiians believed in four other major gods: Kāne, Kanaloa, Ku, and Lono. However, there are dozens, if not hundreds, of other gods. They represent many different aspects of life, including tools, families, objects, professions, plants, and places. There are simply too many to list.

However, here is a short summary of the primary gods:

Kāne	Kāne is the god of the forests and the trees. Kāne is the most revered of all the gods and is placed highest in terms of importance. This is because he is also the god of creation and procreation. He gave life to the dawn, the sun, the sky, and everything that exists.

Kanaloa	Kanaloa is symbolized by an image of a squid or an octopus. These images are typical representations of the seas, the oceans, and maritime activities. Basically, he is the god of the sea.
Kū	Kū was the god of war, conflict, and wood-crafting. There are many beliefs that if you eat foods like coconut, then you are consuming the essence of the god himself, both in terms of physical and spiritual power.
Lono	Lono is the Hawaiian god of the land and is representative of things like fertility, rainfall, music, peace, culture, and agriculture. If you are thinking about anything to do with the land, farming, or natural resources, Lono is the god you should turn to.

If one wished to honor one of the many gods, there were a plethora of temples, monuments, and places of worship one could visit. These were constructed from stone, grass, and wood, although natural caves and other structures were used as well. They would be topped with idols representing the god themselves. There is no doubt that the Hawaiians' beliefs in these gods were behind many of their rituals and celebrations, including but not limited to feasts and athletic contests.

However, this level of belief continued past celebrations and social activities. It also penetrated how Hawaii was run and organized on a political level. This was not necessarily a good thing. As the years passed, the way Hawaiians ran their country became increasingly more destructive and plagued by warfare.

The Legend of Ka'ena Point

There are many, many Native Hawaiian myths and legends, so we will only retell one here. This legend is about the westernmost point of O'ahu. Near this point is a rock called Pohaku o Kauai ("Rock of Kauai").

Long ago, on a stormy night, a baby was born named Haupu. Even though the weather outside was miserable, a rainbow appeared above the house in which the baby was born. It was still there the next day after the storm had dissipated. The people saw this as some kind of sign.

And they were correct to think this. Haupu was incredibly strong, and he became a courageous warrior. He was known throughout all of the islands for his feats of strength and bravery. However, he also had a terrible temper.

One night, a chief of O'ahu named Ka'ena gathered together people and supplies for a fishing expedition at night. Haupu was sleeping when he heard noises out on the water. Half-asleep, Haupu thought it was a group of warriors heading his way to do harm. He ran out to the cliff's edge and picked up a giant boulder. Using his superhuman strength, he heaved the boulder out into the water.

The canoes splintered apart, and many fishermen lost their lives. This included Ka'ena. The impact of the boulder was so strong that the waves washed so much sand onto the shore that it formed a cape. The survivors of the fishing expedition named the point after their chief who had perished.

An aerial photo of Kaʻena. (Credit: Travis Thurston; Wikimedia Commons)

The Way of the Kahuna

One of the most important classes that developed in Hawaii was known as the kahuna. The word kahuna itself basically translates into "expert," but it could have been applied to any field. The term referred to all kinds of professions, including doctors, surgeons, dentists, ministers, priests, and sorcerers. There were kahunas for building canoes and other crafts, as well as kahunas for navigation.

In ancient Hawaii, a kahuna would have been responsible for making sure their area of expertise was taken care of, such as making sure crops grew and houses were sturdily constructed. Some kahunas would have also been responsible for blessing new buildings and ensuring there was good fortune on a construction project. They would have also been responsible for conducting weddings and rituals.

There is a book titled *Tales from the Night Rainbow*, published back in 1986, that recalls oral traditions and stories as described by Native Hawaiians between the years of 1816 and 1931. It is an old book of oral histories from ancient Hawaii. In this book, there are forty types of kahunas listed, with twenty of those belonging to a healing profession alone. This included such things as diagnosing sickness or pain (*kahuna hāhā*) or a medical priest (*kahuna lapaʻau*).

A *kahuna nui* was a high priest, but becoming one was hard. You had to master ten priestly classes in order to earn this label. These included:

ʻAnāʻanā	Someone who practiced a form of prayer that was related to evil sorcery.
Hoʻounāunā	Someone capable of sending spirits to someone else in a bid to cause them illness.
Lapaʻau	Someone involved in healing practices.
Poʻi ʻUhane	Someone capable of capturing spirits for them to carry out a certain task.
Kuhikuhi puʻuone	Someone who was an expert in finding spiritually connected places to build temples.
Kilokilo	A prophet who was capable of predicting the future.
Nānāuli	Someone who could read nature, such as cloud patterns, the direction of the winds, and when it would rain.

This list does not include all ten branches since some of their definitions have been lost to time. If you were able to become a *kahuna nui*, you would live in prestigious and spiritually important places like the Waimea Valley, which is also known as the Valley of the Priests. Oʻahu's largest temple is located in this valley, which shows how religiously significant it was for ancient Hawaiians.

As the years went by and as the outside world began to connect with Hawaii more and more, the word "kahuna" was used to describe priests that came from other countries.

The Distinctive Culture of Hawaii

It is very important to remember that even though the settlers of Hawaii came from Polynesia, the culture that was established on the islands grew more and more distinct over time. The way they functioned, as in how they built their saltwater fisheries, was brilliantly successful, as was their ability to grow food and work the land in a sustainable way.

As you can see from the sections above, the Hawaiians infused creativity into their lives. Their royalty would be decorated with vibrant feathers, and even the common people would dress in relatively glamorous materials that were colorful and expressive, especially compared with other cultures. The gourds, bowls, and containers that the Hawaiians used were intricate and beautifully carved.

This kind of beauty and attention to detail could be found in all aspects of ancient Hawaiian life, and it is what makes this culture and time period so interesting to explore.

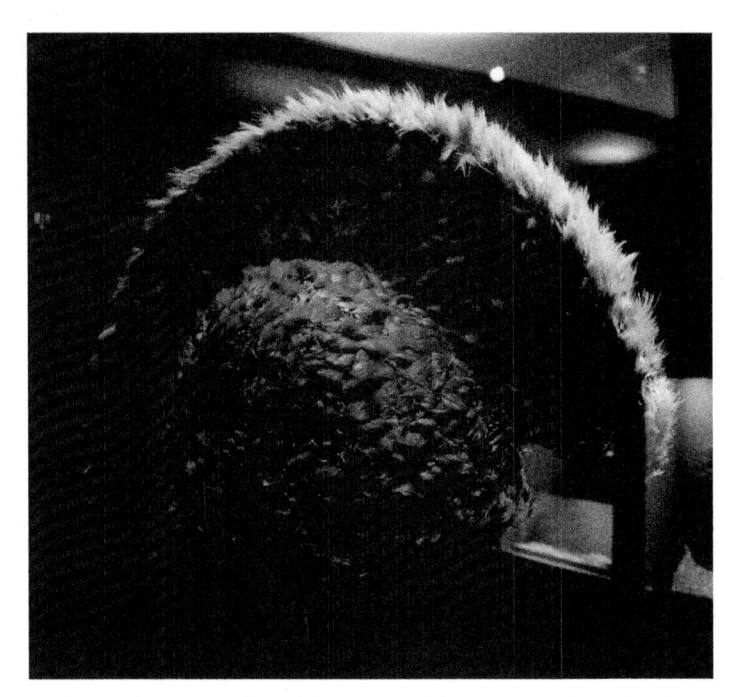

A Hawaiian helm made of feathers, dated sometime before 1779. (Credit: Sailko; Wikimedia Commons)

Life on the Ancient Islands

At this point, you should have a rough idea of what kind of life the ancient Hawaiians led. On a day-to-day basis, they lived and worked alongside each other. They developed a strong belief system and leadership positions. They also figured out how to thrive in their environment.

The ancient Hawaiians lived their lives in pretty much the same way for hundreds of years. That is why we consider ancient Hawaii to stretch from the Polynesians' discovery of the islands in around 400 CE to 1778, which was when James Cook discovered the islands. The years in between saw the Hawaiians setting these systems up, developing the infrastructure, and finding their feet so they could thrive.

But, of course, their way of life would not last that way forever. The major change came when James Cook arrived on the islands.

Hawaii's history is very intertwined with itself, with various significant events overlapping each other, so we will bounce slightly throughout the timeline in the following chapters as we discover what tales unfolded on the islands and what life was like throughout those years.

We will first go to 1778, when Cook discovered the Hawaiian Islands. After this, we will discuss the political situation on the island before Cook arrived and what was going on when he walked upon its shores.

The colonizers of the world were leagues ahead in terms of technology, and Captain James Cook was one of the many explorers who set sail to make new connections and discover new lands. It just so happened that he ventured upon the tropical shores of Hawaii. And with those fateful steps on the sand, the life of Hawaiians would change forever.

The wheels of change had begun to turn, and the archipelago of Hawaii was about to change in a way that nobody could have ever predicted.

Chapter 4 – Europe Makes Contact: 1778

The first European to ever set foot on Hawaii was James Cook. Cook was a captain in the British Royal Navy, and even to this day, he remains one of the most famous explorers to have ever walked the earth. This is the same Captain Cook who charted New Zealand and mapped a way to the eastern coast of Australia. However, one of his biggest discoveries was the Hawaiian Islands, and it was a discovery that would later cost him his life.

James Cook's first voyage took place in 1768. Cook captained the HMS *Endeavour*, and his crew was supposed to chart the course of the planet Venus. They landed on Tahiti in 1769, and from there, he would head to New Zealand. He was the first European to have a conversation with the Māori, although he had help from a Tahitian translator. On his second voyage, which took place from 1772 to 1775, he circumnavigated the planet, becoming one of the first people to cross the Antarctic Circle.

His last voyage set sail in 1776. His goal was to return a Tahitian he had taken during his first voyage. This Tahitian, who was named Omai, enjoyed his time in England very much. He dined with the elite, and his quick wit made him a favorite of the upper crust. Cook was also supposed to keep an eye out for the Northwest Passage on this trip. The Northwest Passage is a North American passage that connects the Atlantic and Pacific Oceans. This legendary passage would be discovered in the 1850s, but it would take another fifty or so years for the passage to be successfully crossed.

So, after dropping Omai off, Cook headed north on the HMS *Resolution*. The HMS *Discovery* also made the trip; it was commanded by Charles Clerke. On January 18th, 1778, James Cook stepped foot on what is now Waimea Harbor, Kaua'i. As far as recorded history is concerned, this was the first time a European stepped on Hawaiian soil.

The interactions were documented by Cook and his crew, and they wrote of how friendly and inviting the Hawaiians were. The Hawaiian tribes greeted the explorers with open arms, and they were, of course, incredibly curious about the ships that had traveled to the islands. After all, they were lovers of the seas and built ships themselves. There was a great interest in how the Europeans had used iron in their ships since Hawaiians were not very familiar with the metal. It is likely they knew of it since debris from shipwrecks would have washed up on their shores, but their knowledge would have been very limited.

Resolution and Adventure with fishing craft in Matavai Bay, *William Hodges, 1776. This is a scene from Cook's second voyage.*

After their initial welcome, James and his crew continued to explore the archipelago and gather as much information on the islands as they possibly could. He dubbed the islands the Sandwich Islands; they were named after the fourth Earl of Sandwich, John Montagu, who was also the first lord of the admiralty. This is also the same man who supposedly invented the sandwich. Cook and his men traveled north to Ni'ihau and then left the islands to head northwest to find the Northwest Passage.

Cook mapped the northwestern coast of North America, but he did not find what he was looking for. In 1779, almost a full year later, Cook returned to the islands of Hawaii, settling down at Kealakekua Bay, which is on the Big Island. This would have only cemented the fact the Hawaiians saw this arrival as a religious event since this was a sacred bay. Kealakekua Bay was deeply connected with the god Lono, who was the god of peace, farming, and fertility.

Native Hawaiians were used to canoes and small boats that were capable of navigating the various islands, but boats designed to the caliber of the HMS *Discovery* would have been utterly mind-blowing, which might have led to the people thinking they were interacting with the gods themselves.

What is more, when James Cook arrived on the islands this second time, he and his men docked at Kealakekua Bay when the Hawaiians were engaged in their annual festival dedicated to Lono. Some scholars state that the Hawaiians saw Cook as an incarnation of Lono; however, there is a lack of evidence that proves this idea.

It is important to remember that Hawaiians would have seen this arrival of the Europeans as a hugely religious event. Since the landing site was considered a sacred place, the Hawaiians would have treated the European explorers as gods. Although some historians today state that the Hawaiians saw Cook as being the god Lono (the Hawaiian god of land), it is important to note that Native Hawaiians today believe that the ancient Hawaiians did not actually think that the Europeans were gods. According to Samuel

Kamakau, a Hawaiian historian who lived in the 1800s, the ancient Hawaiians might have initially thought Cook was Lono but that he soon failed a test, showing he was mortal. "Here is the test of a god: if we tempt them and they do not open their gourd container which holds their ancestral gods, then they are themselves gods, but if they open the sacred gourds [the yield to the temptation of women], then they are not gods—they are foreigners."

The Europeans were still treated very honorably and respectfully, but there is a strong possibility that the ancient Hawaiians knew that these men were not gods. Regardless, they would have done everything they could to make sure their visitors felt welcomed and well looked after. And if they did believe the men were gods, displeasing them would have certainly resulted in negative consequences on an unearthly scale.

Records have documented that the Europeans traded some of their iron nails for sex with Native Hawaiian women. As noted above, ancient Hawaiians had a different outlook on sex than Europeans, who likely viewed the women as "loose." Prostitution was not a thing in ancient Hawaii, so these women were likely not trading their bodies in exchange for sex; the European men likely saw it that way, though. Rather, sleeping with visitors was seen as a way of strengthening ties. As time passed, the women began moving to important trade centers to sleep with the Europeans in exchange for provisions they could not obtain from the islands, which more closely resembles how we view prostitution today.

Cook and the crews of both ships were treated incredibly well, and they enjoyed the attention. They ate all the best food, took the best sleeping places, and indulged in all the sex and other island luxuries they wanted.

There is very little doubt that the Europeans were taking advantage of the Hawaiians and their good nature. This same situation occurred time and time again when Europeans discovered other civilizations as they explored the world. However, this favor could not last forever.

After around a month, one of the European crew members unexpectedly died. The relationship between the Hawaiians and the Europeans became strained after this. Death was obvious proof that the Europeans were mortals and had no connection to the gods. On top of this, they had overstayed their welcome. Sensing the strain in their relationship, Cook decided to leave the islands, setting out from Kealakekua Bay and heading back out onto the ocean.

Yet fate had other ideas. Not even a week passed before the HMS *Resolution* was damaged at sea by storms. Both ships returned to the islands, as the *Resolution* was incapable of traveling. The reception Cook and his crew received this time around was very different from before.

Instead of being greeted with adoration and happiness, the Europeans were welcomed with a barrage of rocks and stones hurled by the natives. The Europeans did not have much of a choice, though, and they stayed on the Big Island to repair the ship. Tensions continued to escalate, and the Hawaiians stole one of the cutter vessels from the HMS *Discovery*. Cook and his men decided to confront the king of the island to negotiate and get the mast back from the Hawaiian natives.

These interactions did not remain peaceful. A lesser Hawaiian chief was shot, and the conflict escalated into an all-out riot. A mob of Hawaiians descended upon the group of Europeans. They used their guns to create a path so they could escape. However, some of the Europeans died, including Cook.

After this, peace was not an option. The *Resolution* shot their cannons while the men on board shot their muskets at the Hawaiians on the shore. This kind of firepower and military might was something they had never witnessed before. More than thirty Hawaiians were said to have died in the conflict.

It took a few days of defending the ships and making the vital repairs that were needed, but eventually, both the *Discovery* and the *Resolution* were able to set sail and venture back home to England.

This story details the first encounter that the Hawaiians had with the larger outside world, and it is clear to see how and why Hawaii became such a turbulent nation. This encounter, in a way, foreshadows the betrayal that Hawaii would later face by outside nations.

After Cook visited the islands, Hawaii would never be the same again. The rest of the world slowly began to hear about this mysterious, tropical paradise, and explorers began to move in. Once the Hawaiians' history began to be written down, it made it easier to decipher what had occurred before Cook and his men arrived on the islands.

Chapter 5 – A Paradise Divided, and the Wars Rage On

Before we get to the significant changes that divided Hawaii and redirected the archipelago forever, we need to rewind a few decades prior to James Cook's arrival to the islands.

Like any nation in the world, Hawaii's population experienced power struggles, civil wars, and political issues. There were frequent fights between territories, some of which even expanded across multiple islands. This was especially the case between Hawaiʻi and Maui.

Now, while this may not have been on the same scale as what was happening in Rome or mainland Europe or even rampaging warlords like Genghis Khan, Hawaii was not a perfect place. There was some kind of order on each island, and the *kapu* kept everyone in check. Later, around 1795, a monarchy was established that reigned over all the Hawaiian Islands for a little over a century.

But in the times of ancient Hawaii, the islands and their people had the power to convene courts that could settle disputes, calm conflicts, and keep everything running smoothly. Remember, this is what Hawaiian life was like for hundreds of years.

Of course, the tools the natives used developed over time to be more efficient, as did the way their housing was built, rituals were carried out, and the way disputes were sorted. However, how far the Hawaiians could evolve was always limited due to their isolation.

Nevertheless, this structure of the monarchy and chiefs was represented on each island, and it was a progressive system that cemented itself into place at the beginning of Hawaiian civilization. However, all this was about to change with the birth of Alapa'inuiakauaua, more commonly referred to as Alapainui or Alapa'i the Great.

While the actual date of his birth is unknown, there is no doubt that this one man and his actions changed the course of Hawaiian history forever.

Scarcity of Records

Before we get into the story of the Kingdom of Hawaii, it is worth explaining that up until this point, it is hard to pinpoint who the leaders were at which time since there was no written documentation or writing of any kind. If we were to look at rulers before Alapainui, there would be a lot of speculation and little information to elaborate on. Much of the information would be a bit dull, as only the most basic information was passed on, or it would contain fantastical tales that are likely not completely true.

We will look at one early ruler as an example of how little we know and how history intertwines with myths. During the late 15th century, the ruler of Hawai'i was Līloa. His compound could be found in the Waipi'o Valley. He had two sons, Hākau and 'Umi-a-Līloa, with his wife Pinea (who was his aunt on his mother's side) and Akahi-a-Kuleana (his lesser wife), respectively. Hākau became the ruler after his father's death, and 'Umi-a-Līloa took that role after he rose up in rebellion against his brother. He went on to unite most of the Big Island.

This is not the most stimulating of reads. However, the succession of Līloa has another story. The Līloa bloodline was said to have gone back as far as Hawaii's creation by the gods, so it is somewhat safe to assume that he was a part of the bloodline that had always held the metaphorical crown of Hawai'i.

The beginning of the story starts the same; Līloa gave birth to two sons. However, 'Umi-a-Līloa did not grow up with his birth father. Instead, his mother hid his royal identity from him. When he became sixteen, his stepfather was about to punish him. His mother said he should not since 'Umi-a-Līloa would one day be chief.

The secret was out, and 'Umi-a-Līloa took the tokens his mother had hid from him and showed them to his true father. Hākau was jealous of the attention 'Umi-a-Līloa received, as Līloa favored him. When Līloa died, the throne passed to Hākau, but 'Umi-a-Līloa was made his advisor.

The hostilities between the brothers were too great, and 'Umi-a-Līloa left with some followers. Over the years, he gathered more men to his side. One day, 'Umi-a-Līloa was walking alone in a forest. But he soon discovered that one of these trees was not a tree but rather a man! This man had to have been at least eleven feet tall. He had been transformed into a giant after eating a fish that had been given to him by a god. He said that 'Umi-a-Līloa would one day be king.

Buoyed by the giant's words, 'Umi-a-Līloa launched a rebellion against his brother, and Hākau was killed. Some say that 'Umi-a-Līloa sacrificed his half-brother to the gods. Regardless of his brother's fate. 'Umi-a-Līloa became the next king of Hawai'i. In fact, he became one of the most honored kings in all of Hawaiian history due to his ability to unite almost all of the districts on the Big Island.

As with most legends, you can find the truth nestled in this story. Many of the more famous rulers have interesting and unique tales about their lives. However, this book is going to retell the more established histories of rulers on Hawai'i, which, unfortunately, is only a handful.

The Dawn of a New Age

Despite the lack of written sources, we do know a bit thanks to word of mouth. These events were passed down until James Cook arrived. These stories might have been told to the newcomers, who then wrote them down, although some of the tales might have been written down later. Scholars have spent time piecing together the facts and figuring out what the most likely course of events was.

We are going to begin with Alapainui, who was born in the late 17th or early 18th century. He was the son of Chief Kauaua-a-Mahi and Chiefess Kalanikauleleiaiwi. When he came of age, he became the chief of Kohala, which can be found in the northwestern regions of the Big Island. He was a chief who answered only to the king of Hawai'i himself. But that was about to change.

During his time as the chief of Kohala, Alapainui was the people's favorite. He was a well-respected ruler who put the people in his region first. His population loved him, cheered for him, and were content under his guidance.

In the late 17th century, the leader of Hawai'i was Keawe'īkekahiali'iokamoku, who was also Alapainui's uncle. He was also favored by the people. He created some semblance of peace on the island through marriage alliances with the chiefs. Keawe'īkekahiali'iokamoku ruled with his half-sister, who was also his wife, Kalanikauleleiaiwi (yes, the same Kalanikauleleiaiwi who was the mother of Alapainui).

When he passed away in 1725, his sons, Kalanike'eaumoku and Kalaninuimamao, fought for the throne. This conflict quickly escalated into a civil war. Alapainui took advantage of the infighting, and he was able to usurp the throne. He took his place as the new king of Hawai'i.

It was a bloody time, as Hawai'i and Maui were fighting with each other. Regardless, the people saw Alapainui as a fantastic leader. He helped to resolve issues quickly and efficiently, and eventually, the two island nations came to terms with each other. But as soon as one conflict dies, another tends to sprout up. During Alapainui's rule, Hawai'i also had to come to grips with its tensions with O'ahu.

Interestingly, however, Alapainui's niece, Keku'iapoiwa II, became pregnant. This child would come to be known as Kamehameha I; this is a name you are going to want to remember. Keku'iapoiwa was said to have had a craving for shark eyeballs while she was pregnant, which was a spiritual sign that her son was to be a killer of chiefs.

Fearful of the prophecy, Alapainui tried to organize the death of the newborn. However, the child was able to escape with the help of Nae'ole, the man who had taken Alapainui's place as the chief of Kohala. Alapainui later changed his mind and was able to reconcile with the child, who would have been about five years old by this time. Alapainui placed him under the care and parental guidance of his first and most favored wife, Keaka.

Alapainui died in 1754, after which he was succeeded by his first son, Keawe'ōpala, who was, in turn, overthrown by Kalani'ōpu'u (full name Kalani'ōpu'u-a-Kaiamamao). Kalani'ōpu'u was the king when Captain James Cook arrived on the island. He greeted Cook personally and gave him fine gifts that were suited for nobility. When James Cook came back to the island after the storm damaged his ship, he tried to kidnap Kalani'ōpu'u to get the stolen cutter vessel back. As you now know, this led to Cook's death.

Kalani'ōpu'u passed away in April 1782, and he was succeeded by his son, Kīwala'ō. His nephew, Kamehameha, was given the spiritual role of being the guardian of Kū, the god of war. And this is where the change of the Hawaiian Islands truly begins.

King Kamehameha: The King of Hawaii

While King Alapainui was respected, loved, and renowned for putting his people first, Kamehameha chose a far more ruthless path regarding how he wanted to rule. Thus began some of the bloodiest and most devastating times in Hawaii's history.

There had already been signs that Kamehameha would be a force to be reckoned with even before his birth. After all, his mother's pregnant cravings included the eyeballs of sharks, which was a portent of doom for chiefs on the island. And when Kamehameha took his position as the king of Hawai'i, this part of the prophecy was already coming true.

Kamehameha was born as early as 1736, and he was one of the greatest leaders in Hawaii's history. So, it should come as no surprise that he would be later dubbed Kamehameha the Great. He was the first king of the Kamehameha bloodline, and his descendants would go on to rule the islands for generations.

In fact, Kamehameha is the king that is predominantly given credit for founding the Kingdom of Hawaii and eventually the unification of all the islands. But we will get to this later. For now, though, understand that this journey was not peaceful, and it affected everyone in the archipelago.

It might be interesting to some to learn that his birth date is disputed. Experts know he was born between 1736 and 1761. Early historians settled on the year of 1758 due to the passing of Halley's Comet. When Kamehameha was born, there were stories of a great star streaking across the sky. However, it seems unlikely this would be the year of his birth. The stories tell of Kamehameha fighting with his uncle; if he was born in 1758, that would make him a child. For the purposes of this book, we are going to stick with the 1736 birth year.

Since Kamehameha might be the killer of chiefs, he was taken away and hidden at birth for his own protection. He spent many of his early years in Waipiʻo and only returned to Kailua when he was five years old. He lived there with his birth parents until his father died, but his *aliʻi* training continued with his uncle.

Many believed that Kamehameha knew that he was destined for great things. By the time James Cook had arrived on the islands for the first time, Kamehameha was already a highly skilled warrior. He might have been one of the deadliest, as he would have proven himself on the battlefield multiple times by the 1770s.

Ever since Kamehameha was young, he had the dream to unite the Hawaiian Islands. He believed it was his destiny, and this is what everyone around him believed as well. After all, his mother had a craving that foretold his fate as a chief killer. And since he was placed in the position of religious guardian to Kū, the Hawaiian god of war, after his father's death, it should really come as no surprise that conflict was in Kamehameha's blood.

There are a lot of details that give the impression that this was the case. One version of Kamehameha's story says that his prophecy would be fulfilled once he lifted the Naha Stone. This stone, which can still be found today outside the front of the Hilo Public Library in Hawaii, held significant spiritual importance. Babies would be placed on the stone after their birth, and if they remained silent, they were considered to be a part of the Naha bloodline. If they cried, then they were cast out. According to legend, the person who could overturn the stone would unify all of the Hawaiian Islands.

After several failed attempts, Kamehameha, at supposedly only fourteen years old, was the first person who was ever able to do this, once again cementing his destiny. If you take a moment to consider how impactful all these signs from the gods would have been to both Kamehameha and anybody who knew him, then it makes sense that his desire to fulfill his destiny would have been almost overwhelming.

A picture of the Naha Stone. (Credit: W. Nowicki; Wikimedia Commons)

But, of course, while one man believed he had to fulfill his prophecy of uniting the islands, some did not agree. They knew their power, influence, and control would be threatened by such an action.

Some of the ruling chiefs of Hawai'i, including Keawe Mauhili and the Mahoe Keoua twins, among several others, rejected this prophecy. They basically denied Kamehameha from uniting the islands. However, five chiefs supported Kamehameha in his endeavors and swore to help him fulfill his dream.

Thus, the island of Hawai'i was divided once more. This led to the Battle of Moku'ōhai, which took place near Kealakekua Bay in Hawai'i in 1782 (now known as Ke'ei). This was the first of Kamehameha's battles to take place. And the battle was ruthless.

The battle began due to Kalani'ōpu'u's son, Kīwala'ō, inheriting the throne. Kīwala'ō's half-brother did not receive anything, which upset him greatly. He began cutting down Kamehameha's sacred coconut trees. Kamehameha, who now had the backing from the other chiefs, felt he had no choice but to take decisive action.

Women and children were guided to Puʻuhonua o Hōnaunau, which was a refuge on the island. It was as if both sides knew how bloody this battle would be.

Chief Kameʻeiamoku, a high chief and trusted counselor of Kamehameha, was the first to be injured. Despite his injuries, he managed to kill Kīwalaʻō after he was knocked down by a sling stone. Kameʻeiamoku then slit Kīwalaʻō's throat. Kamehameha was able to take the iconic ruler's red feather cloak, symbolically securing his position as the leader of Hawaiʻi.

In fact, once the dust settled, it became clear to all that Kamehameha had won the conflict. He secured his position as the leader of the northern and western parts of the island, bar a few independent leaders.

The controlled regions included Kona, Hāmākua, and Kohala. However, Kīwalaʻō's uncle, Keawemaʻuhili, and his half-brother, Keōuakūʻahuʻula, still controlled some of the regions. Keawemaʻuhili had been captured during the battle, but he was able to escape to Hilo. Keōuakūʻahuʻula, the uncle, took charge of Kaʻū.

Over the coming years, there were several smaller battles, all of which Kamehameha dominated. He would kill or capture (and then typically publicly executed) the remaining chiefs who opposed him.

The Olowalu Massacre

It was clear that tensions were rising on the Hawaiian archipelago in the late 1700s.

With news of battles, prophecies, and rising powers spreading around the islands, the common people and their leaders were rightfully worried. The people were scared that their blood would flow next, and their leaders did what they could to keep the peace while holding onto their land and power. It was a time of uncertainty, and it was unlike anything the islands had seen before.

However, there was an unexpected turn from the outside world.

In 1790, a man named Simon Metcalfe landed on Hawai'i. Metcalfe was a fur trader. He had been born in Europe, but he was living in North America at the time. The high seas were like a second home to him, for he spent much of his time sailing around and selling his furs.

In 1789, he had set sail on his ship, the *Eleanora*. It was accompanied by the *Fair American*, which was commanded by his son, Thomas Metcalfe. They had agreed to meet at the Sandwich Islands, which was what the Hawaiian archipelago was known as by the "outside world."

However, their rendezvous did not go according to plan, as the *Fair American* was captured by Spanish ships and taken to San Blas, which can be found today on the Pacific coast of Mexico. Simon and the *Elenora* still arrived to Hawai'i, doing so in January 1790. He and his crew were greeted by Chief Kame'eiamoku, the trusted counselor of Kamehameha who had slit King Kīwala'ō's throat.

Now, it is unclear how their initial interaction went. If we go by past evidence, the Hawaiians would have greeted Metcalfe positively and given him traditional Hawaiian hospitality. However, it seems as if the chief offended Simon Metcalfe in some way. This resulted in him hitting the chief with the hardened end of a long rope that had come from the ship. As you can probably guess, hitting a high chief of Hawaii with a bit of rope is not going to end well.

Metcalfe sailed to Maui to conduct some business. There, one of the smaller boats that was tied to the *Elenora* was stolen by Native Hawaiians. Perhaps unbeknownst to them, there was a man on board the stolen vessel. Angered by the theft, Metcalfe retaliated by firing his musket into the village, killing several Native Hawaiians in the process. He found out that the boat had been taken to Olowalu, a small coastal town on the west coast of Maui, so he sailed there.

After arriving at Olowalu, he soon discovered the stolen boat on the beach but found it had been completely dismantled and torn apart by the natives. The crewman who had been on board had been killed in the process. Metcalfe, who had already killed several residents at the previous village, did not hold back this time.

He turned the ship toward Olowalu after moving all of the cannons onto the same side, the side that faced the coast. He invited the Hawaiians to come trade with him, with many taking him up at the invitation and paddling their canoes to meet him on the ship. However, it was just a ruse. Once the Hawaiians were nearby, he rained fire upon them. It is believed that over one hundred Hawaiians were killed by the cannon barrage.

Metcalfe was satisfied with his vengeance, and he sailed on, anchoring at Kealakekua Bay. Armed with only spears and basic tools, the Hawaiians knew they were no match for Metcalfe's cannons and muskets. They allowed the mooring to take place, leaving the boat and leaving the men to trade in peace.

A few weeks later, Metcalfe's son and the *Fair American* arrived at the archipelago, unaware of everything that had taken place. The Hawaiians were unaware that the ship was commanded by Simon's own son, but they had already decided to take their revenge upon the next foreign ship they spotted. And they did not hesitate. The Hawaiians sailed out to the *Fair American* on their canoes. They boarded the ship and killed nearly everybody on board, including Metcalfe's son. The only survivor was a man named Isaac Davis.

In the meantime, over at Kealakekua Bay, Kamehameha forbade any further interactions with the *Eleanora*, as he was worried the ships were in communication with each other and that more vengeance might be sought. A boatswain from the *Eleanora*, John Young, ventured ashore to see what was going on, but he ended up being taken hostage by Kamehameha's men. Simon

Metcalfe waited a few days to see if Young would return or if the other ship would arrive. Eventually, he had to set sail, not knowing what had happened to either his boatswain, his son, or the other ship.

Kamehameha was given Isaac Davis and the *Fair American*, which was much smaller than the *Eleanora*. Isaac Davis and John Young would act as military advisors and translators in Kamehameha's quest to unite the islands. In addition to these two valuable men, Kamehameha also gained the cannons from the *Fair American*, which will play an important role later on in the story.

As you can see, there were many different conflicts that plagued the islands. However, the real change took place later that same year (1790). It was perhaps one of the most notable events of ancient Hawaiian history.

The Battle of Kepaniwai

This battle is also referred to as the Battle of the Dammed Waters of ʻĪao or the Battle of the Clawed Cliffs. It was, by far, one of the most devastating conflicts of the region, and it is one that many agree was a pivotal point in Hawaii's history.

The bloodshed far outweighed that of the previous conflicts with the foreign European explorers and even internally between the islands. It is renowned by historians for being one of the landmark battles of the region. It was bitterly fought until the end, with devastating losses on both sides.

The year was 1790. King Kahekili II of Maui was visiting Oʻahu, which is located in the north of the archipelago. During the visit, King Kamehameha took the opportunity to land his fleet of boats and soldiers in Kahului, which was not far from the base of ʻĪao Valley, a beautiful, lush valley in western Maui. Kamehameha's army was one of the most aggressive armies to have ever been assembled on the Hawaiian Islands. It consisted of over 1,200 highly skilled warriors, and they wielded spears and other weapons.

They also had canoes, which they used for navigating long distances in a short amount of time. The units were highly mobile and incredibly dangerous, and they were led by King Kamehameha himself, as well as Kekuhaupiʻo, his prized warrior and military trainer.

A picture of ʻĪao Valley today. (Credit: Mark Fickett; Wikimedia Commons)

The men made their way up the western coast of Maui and eventually encountered King Kahekili II's son, Kalanikūpule, and a handful of other Maui chiefs. They had set themselves up to block the entrance of the valley itself.

As it turns out, both armies were fairly evenly matched in terms of skill and collective numbers. The bloodshed that ensued would last for over forty-eight hours. And even after two days had passed, there was still no clear winner.

This is a powerful opportunity to put yourself in the position of the soldiers. Imagine mooring your canoe on the beach and marching with 1,200 of your brothers in arms on either side of you as you make your way across the tropical landscape to the base of ʻĪao Valley. You know you are going to fight to the death under the leadership of Kamehameha, who was going above and beyond to fulfill his destiny. It is an incredible feat of bravery to consider and empathize with. For many today, it is certainly a surreal position to imagine yourself in.

So, after the forty-eight hours had passed, there did not seem to be any sign of surrender from either side. On the break of the third day, King Kamehameha decided to utilize the two cannons he was in possession of. These cannons were named Lopaka and Kalola, and they had been taken from the *Fair American*. Evidence suggests that these cannons were operated by two of Kamehameha's royal advisors, which just so happened to be the Europeans that had been captured: John Young and Isaac Davis.

The results were catastrophic. While none of the Maui chiefs themselves were killed, the cannon barrage decimated the lines of soldiers. There was so much death that it has been said that the river at the bottom of the valley became full of floating bodies. People have even said that the bodies dammed the waters. Those who survived stated that "the river ran red with the blood of the dead."

Fortunately for the *ali'i* of Maui, Chiefess Kalola (the full-blooded sister of King Kahekili II) and her granddaughter Keōpūolani were able to escape the scene. They traveled west through the valley to the settlement of Olowalu and then went north to Lahaina.

However, there were still great losses. The Maui tribes had suffered a decisive defeat. How were soldiers with spears supposed to compete with the might of European military technology? Chiefess Kalola handled the negotiations. She offered up her granddaughter, Keōpūolani, as a tribute of peace and partnership, with the intention that she could marry Kamehameha in the future. At the time, Keōpūolani was only eleven years old.

This was not the only battle taking place on the Hawaiian archipelago. While King Kamehameha was busy attempting to invade Maui, Keōua Kuahu'ula, who was the last independent chief on the island of Hawai'i, had seized this opportunity. With King Kamehameha out of the picture, Chief Keōua Kuahu'ula gathered his men and raided Kamehameha's territories. He then returned to his settlement on the Big Island.

Of course, this did not go unnoticed. Kamehameha was forced to return to the Big Island to deal with the issue, which meant he had to withdraw his troops from Maui. King Kahekili II continued to rule over Maui, and he also acquired cannons of his own. In 1791, Kahekili II took his soldiers and these newly acquired cannons and tried to invade Hawaiʻi as revenge for the warfare. This, however, was in vain.

Kahekili II and his troops were defeated in the waters separating the two islands in a naval battle that became known as Kepuwahaʻulaʻula. Yet, even so, Kamehameha could not take control of Maui entirely. It was not until a civil war broke out on the island in 1794 or 1795, after Kahekili II had died, that Kamehameha was able to make his move.

The invasion and consequential fights became known as the Battle of Nuʻuanu, a fight that Kamehameha would ultimately win.

Chapter 6 – The Battle of Nuʻuanu: 1795

With Kamehameha quickly fulfilling his prophecy of uniting the Hawaiian Islands and becoming the absolute king, the bloodshed was only set to continue. There were plenty of fights, but easily the most notable of all the conflicts, a fight that defined the direction of the islands, was the Battle of Nuʻuanu.

It is hard for historians to pin down exactly what happened during this battle, as there are several conflicting versions of it. After all, in war, the truth is nothing but the stories of the survivors and usually the victors. However, there is a general idea of what happened.

In 1792 (but it could have been any time up until 1794), an English merchant named Captain William Brown moored in the harbors of Honolulu, which is on the island of Oʻahu, the third-largest island in Hawaii and the most populated one. Oʻahu, at the time, was known as "the gathering place." If the tribes, chiefs, and kings needed to resolve an issue, trade, or meet officially for any reason, then this was the place where they would go.

Due to Hawaii's increasing connections to the outside world, specifically with traders coming to swap goods, Captain Brown would often sail to these ports. As a fur and gun trader, O'ahu was an ideal location to stop for supplies while traveling. This was where Kahekili II was reportedly able to acquire cannons of his own.

While Brown captained several vessels during his lifetime, the most notable in Hawaii's history were the *Prince Lee Boo* and the *Jackal*. After landing, he made an agreement with King Kahekili II, saying that he would assist the king with any military affairs he may find himself in as long as he was allowed to moor there and use the port for business reasons. It was a smart move, as Kahekili could use Brown's assistance against Kamehameha's ever-increasing forces.

As news of this spread, Kamehameha reached out to Captain George Vancouver, an officer of the British Royal Navy. In return for Vancouver's help, Kamehameha basically gave the island to Great Britain around the year 1794. This was done under the idea that the British would protect the island for Kamehameha. However, neither Kamehameha nor Kahekili II ever met in person again after these agreements were made. Kahekili II died in mid-1794, and his son, Kalanikūpule, took over O'ahu, which Kahekili had taken before he died. His uncle (although some sources say half-brother), Ka'eokulani, took the reins of Maui and some other smaller islands.

While these two men had their own conflicts and even fought against each other for full control of the islands at times during Kahekili's lifetime, they put their differences aside and mourned the passing of him together. However, after the two parted ways, Ka'eokulani soon uncovered a plot that his head chiefs were going to throw him off his ship. In response, he convinced his chiefs to join him in going to war against Kalanikūpule.

This was a smaller war, at least compared to the larger one involving Kamehameha. It started around November 16th, 1794, and lasted less than one month. Ka'eokulani commanded his men to march across O'ahu to where he knew Kalanikūpule's men were stationed. However, once they found his army, they were also greeted with the artillery from Captain Brown's ships, which obviously decimated the units on sight.

Devastated with unimaginable losses, those who survived managed to somehow escape, fleeing into the valleys and mountains. However, while Kalanikūpule had won the conflict, this caused an entirely new set of problems. After a disagreement with Captain Brown, Kalanikūpule and his troops killed Brown and a number of his men and took control of both the *Prince Lee Boo* and the *Jackal*.

With weapons, men, resources, and recent victories under their belts, there is little to no doubt that Kalanikūpule would have felt indestructible. Just three weeks later, he and his men set sail toward Hawai'i with all the ships and canoes they could find. They intended to put down Kamehameha's efforts at long last and ultimately decide who the true king of Hawai'i would be.

But it was not to be. The surviving men from Brown's crew managed to take back both ships while they were anchored off the coast of Waikiki, a coastal town in the south of O'ahu. With the ships commandeered, they then sailed off to inform King Kamehameha about everything that was going to happen.

Kamehameha seized the opportunity. He traded supplies for all of Kalanikūpule's weapons that had been stocked on the vessel. Soon after this, he began his assault on O'ahu.

Kalanikūpule was not kept out of the loop. After hearing the news that the assault was on its way, he set up several fortifications on O'ahu. He already had possession of a considerable number of weapons from the Europeans, such as muskets and cannons, but Kamehameha's inventory far outweighed his own. Kalanikūpule knew he was going to be severely outgunned. They were effectively scraping the barrel for supplies in comparison.

Even though one of Kamehameha's chiefs, a man named Kaʻiana, defected to Kalanikūpule's side before the battle began, they knew their chances of winning were slim. It has been rumored that Kaʻiana had become slightly undesirable to Kamehameha. Once he was taken out of Kamehameha's inner circle, he feared that he would be killed, exiled, or be subjected to some other plot against him, so he decided to flee for his life.

During the crossing to the main island for Kamehameha's assault on Oʻahu, Kaʻiana steered his boat away from the main fleet and instead landed on the northern side of the island. Kaʻiana and his troops started to dig into the mountainside of Nuʻuanu Pali, a cliff that was a part of the Koʻolau Range. These holes would act as gunports for Kalanikūpule's men and his cannons.

Even with the help of Kaʻiana, Kalanikūpule and his men were under-prepared and ill-equipped. Kamehameha and his forces had only grown over the last few years, and many were fearful that to stand against him meant they were standing against the prophecy that the islands would be unified under one leader. This was a prophecy set forward by the gods themselves. Kamehameha was prepared, and he believed he was fulfilling his destiny.

Of course, the people of the islands were divided. Some believed in the power of the prophecy and wanted to see it fulfilled. Others believed but did not like Kamehameha and would rather have another leader in his place. Most of the people on both sides were just fearful that their communities, families, and way of life were being threatened and that everything was going to change.

Either way, there was no doubt in anyone's mind that war was coming, which manifested itself in the Battle of Nuʻuanu.

Come February 1795, Kamehameha had managed to assemble the largest army the islands had ever seen, totaling over 12,000 men and over 1,200 canoes. The troops were armed with muskets and cannons, far more than any other army in the archipelago. What is more, John Young had even taken the time to train Kamehameha's men in how to use the weapons properly, making them the most ruthless warriors in the region.

Kamehameha advanced his troops quickly toward the islands of Maui and Molokaʻi, taking control over these regions with relative ease. A few weeks later, he advanced to Oʻahu, and the infamous battle began.

The Fight for the Fulfilled Prophecy

The battle began soon after Kamehameha landed his troops on the southeastern shores of Oʻahu, right near the Waiʻalae and Waikiki regions, which are both near Honolulu. The troops rested for a couple of days, gathering the necessary supplies after their voyage to the island, as well as gathering intel via scouting missions to see what Kalanikūpule had set up.

Once they were ready, they marched west. They first made contact with Kalanikūpule's troops that had been stationed at the Punchbowl Crater. The crater is the extinct tip of the volcano, right in the center of where Honolulu is today.

Kamehameha strategically split his forces in two, sending half of his army around the crater's edge in a flanking maneuver while the other marched directly toward Kalanikūpule and his troops. Almost immediately, Kalanikūpule and his troops were overwhelmed by the pressure coming in from both sides, and he was forced to retreat to his next line of defense, which had been set up in Laʻimi.

Of course, Kamehameha was not going to let this opportunity go to waste, and he pursued his enemy. However, being the strategic master that he was and having the information from the scouting mission prior to the fighting, he dispatched a secret unit of troops up into the Nuʻuanu Valley to clear out the cannon and gun placements that Kalanikūpule and his men had set up earlier.

Once the cannons were cleared, Kamehameha brought forward his own cannon forces to rain terror on Laʻimi. During this fight,

Kalanikūpule was wounded, and the defecting chief, Kaʻiana, lost his life. With the leadership ranks of Kalanikūpule's army falling apart, chaos ensued among the ranks.

Oʻahu's defending army had to run for their lives into the Nuʻuanu Valley, where they were pushed north toward Nuʻuanu Pali. Sadly, this cliff is known for being over one thousand feet high; it is basically a sheer drop to the roaring ocean waves that crash against the rocks below. A choice lay before Kalanikūpule's men. Should they take the plunge or see what Kamehameha's army of skilled and brutal warriors had in mind instead?

A photograph of Nuʻuanu Pali. (Credit: Lukas; Wikimedia Commons)

It is believed that many of Kalanikūpule's warriors jumped to their deaths or were pushed over the edge of the cliff by other terrified soldiers in their panic to retreat from Kamehameha's approaching forces. A century later, around 1898, a team of construction workers who were a part of the building crew for the Pali Road discovered over eight hundred skulls. They are believed to be the remains of those whose lives ended during this era-defining battle.

And thus, with Kaʻiana, the last of the defecting chiefs, dead, and Kalanikūpule missing, injured in action, the battle was swayed in Kamehameha's favor. Thus, he had control over Oʻahu. He was yet another step closer to unifying the islands and fulfilling his destiny.

Of course, not long after the battle was over, Kalanikūpule was found. He was captured by Kamehameha's forces and was ultimately sacrificed to the gods. His death caused the fall of Maui. From this moment, news of the battles and the word of the new leadership spread across the islands. For the first time in history, the archipelago was referred to as the Kingdom of Hawaii.

But alas, despite the victory and being one step closer to having fulfilled his destiny, Kamehameha was not yet finished. There was still much work to do in order to complete his mission. As one might imagine, the stories of the fighting, the power that Kamehameha held, and the fact he was succeeding in what he had set out to do caused a stir among the other island chiefs and the people under their rule.

At this point, Kamehameha still had to capture and control the remaining islands of significance: Kauaʻi and Niʻihau. On top of this, there was an uprising on Oʻahu that needed to be dealt with. Nevertheless, the Kingdom of Hawaii was one step closer to being established.

Chapter 7 – The Birth of the Kamehameha Dynasty: 1810

Some fifteen years passed, and Kamehameha had been hard at work ensuring that the Kingdom of Hawaii would become and remain the powerhouse that he had always envisioned. He wanted it to be the kingdom that the gods had foretold he would rule. With the remaining chiefs, kings, and other regional leaders either dead, sacrificed, or surrendering to him and his forces, the Kingdom of Hawaii was nearly complete by 1810.

Over on Kaua'i, the leader, King Kaumuali'i, had been subjected to raids from Kamehameha over the years, but all of them had failed. He decided to negotiate with Kamehameha and surrender peacefully to avoid the loss of life. It was tempting to kill Kaumuali'i, as Kamehameha had gotten rid of most of the other opposing chiefs. But Kamehameha was a bit reluctant this time around. However, even the other nobles agreed that Kaumuali'i needed to go and pushed Kamehameha to take decisive action. Isaac Davis warned Kaumuali'i beforehand, and Kaumuali'i left, going home to Kaua'i. So, instead of killing Kaumuali'i, the nobles killed Davis.

And so, with the last remnants of rebellion eradicated from the lands, the unification of the islands was complete. The Kingdom of Hawaii rose from the ashes, and future generations would refer to the ruling family as the Kamehameha dynasty.

Perhaps Kamehameha's most notable actions after unifying the islands were ensuring that the islands would remain united and that the empire he created would remain standing even after his death. Some of these steps included actions like unifying the legal system so that the laws of Hawaii were the same throughout the kingdom; before this, the laws changed depending on which island you were on. Kamehameha also set up systems that allowed products that were created on the islands to be used to promote international trading with faraway lands via trade routes. These routes were mainly with the United States and mainland Europe.

Both Davis and Young had become close advisors to King Kamehameha and helped Kamehameha connect with foreign trade routes and governing bodies. They were also of great use to Kamehameha from a military standpoint since they knew how the advanced European weaponry worked. This ensured that Kamehameha's forces remained the most dominant force. After Davis died, Young took care of his children. He treated them as if they were his own, and he evenly divided his lands between Davis's children and his own.

Kamehameha settled into his new position as the leader of the Hawaiian Islands. He was also seen as a religious leader, one very much associated with the god of war, Kū. But as the years passed and as Hawaii became increasingly connected to the outside world, other religions, mainly Christianity, were encouraged by European explorers who came to the islands.

However, King Kamehameha insisted that he would worship the traditional Hawaiian gods and told tales of how he had the power of the gods behind him. After all, he had managed to fulfill his destiny and unite the islands, thus becoming a powerful leader.

News of this conqueror spread so much that powerhouse empires like Great Britain did not send missionaries to the islands as they had with other countries since they believed Kamehameha's devotion to his own gods was too strong.

From the unification of the islands until his death in 1819, Kamehameha worked hard to secure his family's future and the future of the Kingdom of Hawaii. As stated above, the Hawaiian Islands had always remained relatively the same since it was first settled all those years ago. But now, with the changing ways of the world, it was extremely unlikely that it was ever going back.

The Later Years of Kamehameha I

Despite being aggressive in his efforts to achieve unity, Kamehameha lived a mostly peaceful life once he had secured his position as the king of all Hawaii. He worked on the laws of the kingdom and came up with new, innovative ways of bringing the people of the islands together so they could prosper.

After 1812, Kamehameha spent most of his days in the compound he and his family built. The compound was in Kailua-Kona, which could be found at the northern tip of Kailua Bay, Hawaii.

As was the tradition at the time, he lived there with his many wives and children. Modern experts say Kamehameha could have had as many as thirty wives, and it is believed he had children with around eighteen of them. When it comes to his children, it has been said that he had around seventeen sons and eighteen daughters. This means he had about thirty-five children in total, and interestingly enough, he outlived over half of them.

The rest of his life was fairly peaceful. The occasional rebellion likely sprang up, but if it did, it was easily squashed. Kamehameha spent most of his time ensuring the islands would remain united after his death, which occurred sometime between May 8th and May 14th, 1819.

His body became the responsibility of his good friends, Hoapili and Hoʻolulu. They disposed of his body in accordance with the rules of the *hūnākele*. This was a custom in which a sacred body was to be hidden. By hiding the body, the power of the deceased's soul and being, their mana, would be preserved and kept away from those who did not possess the same power or purity. Kamehameha was put to rest in a hidden location. To this day, we do not know where he was buried.

Years later, King Kamehameha III (r. 1825-1854), the child of Kamehameha I, asked Hoapili to show him the resting place of his father's bones, but they were not able to undertake the journey out of fears of being followed by others who might harm the body.

The Death of the *Kapu*

Since nearly the beginning of Hawaiian culture, the people of the islands were governed by what was known as the *kapu*, which can be viewed as the ancient Hawaiian code of conduct. The *kapu* system was present in every single aspect of Hawaiian life, from gender roles, the politics of the islands, and even religion.

The people followed the *kapu*, and they did so even when the European settlers landed on the islands. To go against the *kapu* was a serious offense punishable by death. As mentioned before, the Hawaiians believed in mana, which is essentially a person's life essence, power, or soul. Kamehameha was rich with mana, but an average person may have only had an average amount of mana or perhaps even none at all. To go against or break the teachings of the *kapu* would mean damaging your spiritual power, making you a threat to other people's mana, hence why it was punishable.

The concept of *kapu* was not unique to Hawaii; it actually exists throughout many Polynesian cultures. Within these communities, it is known as taboo, tapu, or tabu. The Hawaiian word *kapu*, along with these other words, can be translated as "forbidden," but it can also mean "sacred," "keep out," or "no trespassing."

The *kapu* applied differently to the ranks in Hawaiian society. For example, a series of restrictions known as the *Kapuhili* were invoked when anybody came into contact with a chief or king, but it could also apply to anyone with a high level of spiritual power. Let us say you were a common person, and you were called in front of a chief. The *Kapuhili* meant you could not come in contact with his hair, come in contact with his fingernail clippings, or look directly at him. You had to remain in sight of him while you were in his presence with at least one head height above him.

To go against these rules was punishable as per the guidelines of the *kapu*. The highest-ranking members of society, such as a king, had to wear red and yellow feathers as a sign of their rank. For anybody else to wear such feathers would be punishable.

However, understanding when and where the *kapu* applied was made clear wherever you went. For example, to enter a chief's personal space and carry out one of the above crimes would be punishable, but the space would have to be marked to say that the *kapu* was enforced there. This was usually done using *Pahu Kapu*, which is an image or engraving of two crossed staffs with a white ball on top of each one. These would be set up outside the homes or compounds of the chiefs and kings, making it clear it was a *kapu* space.

Another form of the *kapu* was the *'Ai Kapu*, which defined how men and women were supposed to interact with each other. Through the *'Ai Kapu*, the *ali'i* (the nobles of Hawaii) were able to keep their power.

The *'Ai Kapu* was responsible for some of the restrictions we talked about earlier in the book, such as the fact that men and women could not eat together. What is more, certain foods were restricted for women, such as pork, which was regarded as being the physical form of the god Lono. Types of fruit were also forbidden, such as most varieties of bananas and coconuts. These fruits were known as being the body of the gods Kanaloa and Kū, respectively.

Taro was also considered a sacred food (it was considered to be the body of Kāne). Women were prohibited from not only eating these but also interacting with products from these fruits, such as coconut rope. Therefore, it was *kapu* for women to prepare, touch, or cook with these foods.

It is important to have an understanding of *kapu* since it was how Hawaii was run and organized since the early days. However, once Kamehameha unified the islands and became the leader of the lands, the *kapu* slowly began to be pushed to the side.

However, it was not Kamehameha the Great who ended it. His son, who was also named Kamehameha, was the one to abolish it. The year 1819, the same year Kamehameha I died, was when the laws began to shift. Kamehameha II made the changes, along with his mother, Queen Keōpūolani. Another one of his father's wives, Ka'ahumanu, and Kahuna-Nui Hewahewa (one of the leading religious leaders at the time) were also involved.

On one fateful day, the four of them sat down together and ate a meal that consisted of forbidden foods, thus going against the *kapu* and effectively breaking its power. Up until that moment, the way the *kapu* was enforced gave power to rulers and chiefs all over the islands; in other words, it gave them power over the people. The chiefs and kings would make the decisions and take action according to the rules of the *kapu*. Now, though, the leading royal family was diminishing the *kapu's* importance.

With the *kapu* effectively abolished, the Kamehameha bloodline gained more powers as the definitive rulers of the islands, and it gave less power to the rulers and chiefs who operated below them. Thus, the political ruling system that had given the chiefs power and a degree of prestige was gone. The ruling Kamehameha family, alongside their advisors and inner circle, was now the dominant force of power.

The Law of the Splintered Paddle

While the abolition of the *kapu* was a definitive change in the way Hawaii was run, the shift in the power structures had started long before that symbolic meal. In fact, it started as far back as 1797 after Kamehameha was well on his way to unifying all the islands.

After the war, Kamehameha was on a military visit to Puna, one of the southern districts on the Big Island. While there, he came across a group of civilians working on the beach, and a conflict arose. During the fighting, Kamehameha chased two fishermen, and he caught his leg on a piece of reef and fell. One of the fishermen turned and smashed Kamehameha over the head with a boat paddle, shattering it into pieces.

Kamehameha could have been killed there and then, but for some reason, despite having been chased, the fisherman spared Kamehameha's life. Some years later, the same fisherman was brought before King Kamehameha.

However, instead of condemning the man to death, Kamehameha spared his life. He exclaimed to the court that the fisherman was an inspiration and had only been acting to protect his family as any man should. Because of this, the Law of the Splintered Paddle, also known as the Kānāwai Māmalahoe, was created.

It read:

"E nā kānaka,

E mālama 'oukou i ke akua

A e mālama ho'i ke kanaka nui a me kanaka iki;

E hele ka 'elemakule, ka luahine, a me ke kama

A moe i ke ala

'A'ohe mea nāna e ho'opilikia.

Hewa nō, make."

Translated into English, this reads:

"Oh, people,

Honor thy god;

respect alike [the rights of] people both great and humble;

May everyone, from the old men and women to the children

Be free to go forth and lie in the road

Without fear of harm.

Break this law, and die."

This is such an important law, especially the line "from the old men and women to the children/Be free to go forth and lie in the road." If we translated this into modern terms, the law would read something like, "Let every elderly person, woman, and child lie by the roadside in safety." This means the king would provide for the people's needs and grant them safety. The same phrase is immortalized in the State Constitution of Hawaii (Article 9, Section 10), and it has even become a model for modern-day human rights legislation within the state.

However, it is important to note that Kamehameha did not create these laws; rather, he combined concepts that had been around for generations and put them into one diplomatic notion. Years before this law passed, chiefs in Hawaii's long history were executed publicly when they mistreated the common people under their rule. Hawaiians were renowned for being intolerant of bad leaders and corruption. This was one of the reasons why Kamehameha was able to get his power in the first place.

Therefore, it is clear that by making this law, Kamehameha strategically put himself in a favorable position with the people of the future Kingdom of Hawaii. Making such a change in the law meant that there was less of a chance of bad leaders having the power to do anything that impacted the people negatively; thus, the common people were better off because of it. This meant fewer civil wars and rebellions and more people who were content with the government.

Some fun facts surround this law, showing just how much it impacted modern Hawaiian society. You can find variations of this law in Hawaiian culture, including the aforementioned human rights laws, laws for protecting the elderly, children's rights, homeless initiatives, and even when it comes to bicyclist safety. And if you look at the badge of the Honolulu Police Department, right in the center, you will see a symbol of two crossed paddles, a nod at the law that was devised all those years ago.

And so, with the Kamehameha bloodline in power, the islands unified, and the prophecy fulfilled, the Kingdom of Hawaii was, at last, entering a time of peace and prosperity.

Chapter 8 – The End of Ancient Hawaii

This peace did not last.

The first Christian missionaries arrived on the islands soon after the symbolic meal that broke the *kapu* traditions apart and changed Hawaii and its culture forever. The year was 1820, and despite the hundreds of years that Hawaii had spent in relative isolation, the rest of the world had other ideas.

Hawaii now had connections to the outside world, as we have explored previously. Traders and explorers would pass the islands every now and then, stopping for rest, trading supplies with each other, and then moving on. Due to the Hawaiians' dedication, they held on to their gods and way of life.

However, as time passed, vessels from other nations became increasingly commonplace, as the entire world was becoming increasingly connected via shipping and trade routes. Hawaii would not be left out.

Around 1893, American colonists were in full control over the sugar-based economy that had been created throughout the islands. It was the primary driving force of the economy, and it had integrated itself into every aspect of Hawaii's life and culture. While Hawaii had managed to remain independent for so many centuries, the time to transform with the rest of the modern world had come.

But we are getting ahead of ourselves a bit here. Let us start at the beginning with the missionaries.

The Beginning of the End Started with One Man

It all started with one man named Henry Ōpukahaʻia, a young Hawaiian born around 1792 in Nīnole, Hawaiʻi, and there is no doubt that he had very little idea how much he was about to change the future of Hawaii throughout his life.

While there is little recorded evidence for what Ōpukahaʻia's early life was like (he would go by Henry later on in life), it is suggested he lived in his hometown on the Big Island. From diary entries and other self-recorded evidence from later in his life, we can ascertain that both of his parents died around 1800. He was only ten or so at the time. Somehow, he was able to escape the relentless might of the forces with his baby brother hanging onto his back, who unfortunately died after being hit with a spear during their attempt to flee.

However, Ōpukahaʻia survived, and he was even adopted by the same warrior who had killed his parents. This guardianship would last just over a year and a half. During these eighteen months, Ōpukahaʻia discovered that his uncle was a kahuna at one of the nearby religious temples.

Through his uncle, he was able to contact the rest of his family and ultimately went to live with his grandmother and uncle. One day, he decided to visit one of his aunts in a nearby village. During his visit, his aunt was suddenly taken by soldiers for an infraction against the *kapu* and was put to death.

Even though he had been taken by surprise, Ōpukahaʻia was able to escape once again. He allegedly squeezed through a hole in the side of the house and then watched helplessly as the soldiers threw his aunt over the edge of a nearby cliff. Of course, this is a traumatic experience for anyone to go through, especially one who could remember the murder of his parents. There is no doubt that these memories stayed with Ōpukahaʻia for his entire life.

He eventually returned home to his uncle, where he dedicated his life to learning about the rituals of the temple so that he could one day become a kahuna and take his uncle's place. However, this was not the life that Ōpukahaʻia was destined for. And it seems he knew it as well. Later on, Ōpukahaʻia would learn to read and write, and he wrote of his experiences while learning with his uncle. In his memoir, he wrote, "I began to think about leaving that country to go to some other part of the world...probably I may find some comfort, more than to live there without a father or mother."

This was a powerful thought, and it was one he acted on. The moment the *Triumph*, an English trading vessel, moored in Kealakekua Bay, Ōpukahaʻia spontaneously made his way on board and introduced himself. The vessel was captained by Caleb Brintnall, who also invited another young Hawaiian boy named Hopoʻo on board to stay for dinner. Neither boy spoke English, but they both stayed for dinner and spent the night on the ship.

Because of their good manners and young age, both boys were invited to stay on the vessel, which means they were given the interesting opportunity of sailing the ocean. They traveled around the Pacific, went around the Cape of Good Hope in South Africa, and landed in New York in 1809. And Ōpukahaʻia did all this around the age of sixteen. He was about to do something that few Native Hawaiians had done at this point in time.

It was on this voyage that Ōpukahaʻia began to be called Henry. It is possible the sailors had a hard time pronouncing his name or perhaps did not care enough to learn it. But the name Henry stuck since the sailors called him this. Both the boys barely considered what this meant and agreed to set sail with him.

Equally as important, Ōpukahaʻia was introduced to a fellow sailor on the ship. His name was Russell Hubbard, and he taught Ōpukahaʻia the English language. Hubbard took the time to teach him how to read and write, and he often used the Bible as a text to assist with these lessons. This was Ōpukahaʻia's first introduction to the Bible, which had a profound impact on him.

Ōpukahaʻia more than likely began to embrace the name Henry due to these lessons. After all, his native gods of Hawaii and even the culture of the islands had brought him nothing but pain and suffering. He lost his family due to wars and silly (at least in his eyes) infractions of the *kapu*. His childhood had been harsh and bleak. But sailing on this vessel allowed him to see that his future could be bright, and his dreams could be endless. It is no wonder he was so captivated by this new way of looking at the world.

A watercolor of Greenwich Street, New York, 1810. (Credit: New York Public Library)

Once the crew had docked in New York, the ship was sold, and a merchant took both the Hawaiian boys home for dinner. Take a moment to put yourself in the shoes of Henry and Hopoʻo. You would have spent all your life on a tropical island, surrounded by nothing but sand, trees, the ocean, and close-knit communities. Your whole life was then transported across the ocean to a vibrant city teeming with people, horses, sights, and sounds that would have been dizzying, to say the least. Suffice it to say that it would have been nothing short of mind-blowing.

Picture stepping through the door into the merchant's house. This building would have been filled with so many rooms and other luxury items that it would have been beyond comprehension. Usually, ancient Hawaiian homes had a rather open-plan approach, with four basic walls and everything included on the inside—except for kitchens.

Henry and Hopoʻo would have been fascinated by the fact that the food was cooked indoors. Furthermore, this would have been taking place around the same time, if not before, the *kapu* was dissolved, meaning Henry would have only ever known life with the *kapu* enforced. This meant that women and men sitting around having dinner at the same table would have been completely surreal for him.

This was Henry's first experience with New York and the American/European lifestyle. He continued to live with Captain Brintnall and his family, but after a short time in New York, the family moved to New Haven, Connecticut. While living there, Henry met Edwin Dwight, who was attending Yale University. Henry wanted to master the English language, but his lessons with Brintnall were not proving fruitful enough. Dwight recognized his plight and sent him over to one of his relatives, Timothy Dwight IV (he was also the founder of the American Board of Commissioners for Foreign Missions, which was one of the first American missionary organizations). Henry's knowledge of English would rapidly enhance with Timothy Dwight, who was a much better teacher than Brintnall.

With this doorway opening in his life, Henry became very involved with Christianity. The more he learned, the more he began to leave his past Hawaiian religion behind, and the more he started to focus on the Christian God. In one written passage in his memoirs, which he had started writing in an attempt to improve and master his developing English skills, he wrote, "Hawai'i gods. They wood-burn. Me go home, put 'em in fire, burn 'em up. They no see, no hear, no anything. We make them [idols]. Our God—he make us."

As he continued to live with his new family, his faith became more and more ingrained. This heavily religious family pushed him even further into religious studies and pursuits, with Henry dedicating time every morning and every evening to prayers.

As the years passed, Henry lived an increasingly varied life in the United States. He moved around a fair amount, traveling to places like Torrington and other cities throughout Connecticut, as well as a few in New Hampshire. He typically worked on farms, learning how to plant, till the soil, and harvest crops, but he also made sure to get involved with local church groups.

Before 1814, he had begun speaking publicly in front of crowds about his Lord and Savior. He also began translating the Bible into Hawaiian and even creating a dictionary for the Hawaiian language.

During this time, he found himself talking with Christian missionary groups. And he was not the only Native Hawaiian interested in spreading the word of God; there were other Polynesians as well as Native Americans who wanted to take up this mantle. Of course, today, we could look at these actions with a different lens. These young boys were introduced to an attractive culture, with many of them likely seeking different answers to what had happened to them during their lives. Christianity offered that answer. These missionaries likely knew that native believers in Jesus could spread the ideas of the faith better than they could, so they encouraged their interest in further spreading the Gospel.

In 1816, the Foreign Mission School was created. This school was focused on turning people of non-Christian societies into missionaries. Of course, this idea excited Henry, so he jumped at the chance to help them achieve this goal, believing that Hawai'i could massively benefit from the introduction of Christianity.

By 1817, a mission group of twelve students, with half of them being of Hawaiian descent, had been formed. They were training at the Foreign Mission School in Cornwall, Connecticut, where they learned how to become missionaries. However, within a year of securing his place on the mission, Henry became drastically ill. He was soon diagnosed with typhus fever.

Although he was treated, the treatment did not work in the long run. Henry continued to lose his strength, and on February 17th, 1818, he passed away. He was only twenty-six years old. The doctor's note describes how peacefully he passed, with the statement detailing how he died with "a heavenly smile on his face." In his later translated memoir, his last words were, "My love be with you."

We know about the stories described above because of this memoir Henry had left behind. Nearly all of his experiences were recorded in his diary. These texts are an incredibly detailed account of his life, his journeys, and how he thought and felt about his faith. The book was titled *The Memoirs of Henry Obookiah*. As you know, his name was not Obookiah; it was Ōpukahaʻia. However, that was not how English people spelled and pronounced his name since most of them were not able or willing to understand non-English languages at the time. Henry was buried in a cemetery in Cornwall, Connecticut.

The diary he wrote was published soon after his death, and it quickly inspired fourteen missionaries to embark on a mission to the Hawaiian Islands. Among them was a man named Samuel Ruggles. He was the only one who had met Henry face to face before his death. On top of this, Henry's work on creating a dictionary for the Hawaiian language and a translated Bible gave other missionaries a foundation for the first Hawaiian primer.

Although Henry never made it back to Hawaiʻi, his influence on missionary work on the Hawaiian Islands cannot be understated. And the people of Hawaiʻi eventually wanted him to be buried on the island. In 1993, a group of his descendants took his body from the cemetery his body resided in (located in Cornwall) back home to the Big Island. He was buried in Kahikolu Cemetery in Napoʻopoʻo.

There is even a plaque in the cemetery that marks the spot where he was buried. It is looked after to this day by the Ka ʻOhe Ola Hou, an organization set up to further Christian teachings on the island. In fact, this organization's origins date all the way back to that first missionary venture. Unfortunately, Henry would never learn about the impact he had on his native homeland, nor would he have any idea of what scale the impact would be.

The Land That Changed Forever

The date is now October 23rd, 1819.

A group of missionaries working for the Pioneer Company of American Protestants set sail on the *Thaddeus*. They were heading for the Kingdom of Hawaii. The journey took an estimated 160 days, but they finally saw the islands on March 30th, 1820. They moored at Kailua-Kona, a small coastal town in the west of the Big Island, on April 4th.

Their mission? To make people, regardless of class, knowledgeable and happy. To do this, they planned to introduce the natives to the Christian God.

This was the mission Samuel Ruggles went on. And it was led by Hiram Bingham. Today, he is remembered for introducing Christianity to the Hawaiian Islands. He is known for influencing the Hawaiians' view on Catholicism. Due to his encouragement, Catholic Hawaiians were persecuted on the islands.

The arrival of the missionaries was devastating. When James Cook arrived on the islands all those years ago, he brought diseases. Most of these were sexually transmitted diseases, although some contend that the Hawaiians had already encountered some of these diseases due to trading with other Polynesian islands. However,

Cook and his men seemed to spread the diseases faster than before. There were some diseases that caused death, but for the most part, the diseases Cook's men spread tended to cause infertility.

The missionaries, on the other hand, as well as other foreigners arriving on the islands, brought more deadly diseases, namely measles and leprosy. Other diseases included influenza, cholera, mumps, and tuberculosis.

While it is unclear what the total population of Hawaii was before all these foreigners arrived, it is believed that by the end of the 1800s, the Hawaiian population was only around thirty-nine thousand people. This means the diseases took tens of thousands of lives, perhaps even close or over one hundred thousand.

It is worth noting that Westerners often did not see the devastating death rate as a result of the Hawaiians' lack of immunity. Rather, they thought it demonstrated how dirty the Hawaiians were and how much they needed Western culture in their lives so they could thrive.

Between the years of 1820 and 1863, which became known as the "Missionary Period," over 180 men and women traveled to the Hawaiian Islands. On these missionary ventures, there was a selection of people who would fulfill certain roles. These ranged from teachers and printers to bookbinders, gospel leaders, and even farmers. The vast majority of these people were in their early twenties, meaning they were very energetic and passionate about the cause they were serving, making it much more likely that people would convert.

During the earlier missions, the missionaries focused on the most important communities on the islands and set up stations that would be home to the churches and schools they could use for teaching and religious purposes. By 1850, eighteen stations had been constructed, with six of them on the Big Island alone. The main buildings were originally constructed using traditional thatched methods, like the surrounding Hawaiian buildings, but they were later constructed or upgraded using stone and wood materials. This made them far more impressive than Hawaii's native infrastructure and seemingly more appealing to those in the neighborhoods.

Some of the more notable churches include Mokuʻaikaua Church. This church was founded by Reverend Asa Thurston and his wife, Lucy. The building was completed in 1837, and it remains standing to this day. It is the oldest Christian church on the islands.

A picture of Mokuʻaikaua Church today. (Credit: W. Nowicki; Wikimedia Commons)

Samuel Ruggles set up his own church on the islands with his wife, Nancy, and another couple, Sam and Mercy Whitney. This was built during Samuel's voyage to the islands in 1819/20, and he would spend most of the rest of his life traveling between the islands. The Waimea Mission Church began to be constructed in the 1830s. Interestingly, the first service in this church took place in 1854 before the building was even finished.

The last church we will mention is Kawaiahaʻo Church, which translates as "the water of Haʻo." Its name refers to the sacred water springs that can be found on the church grounds. The church was made from coral materials and was completed in 1842. Of course, many other churches were constructed, along with the houses that the missionaries lived in, all of which would have out-scaled the Native Hawaiian architecture.

A picture of Kawaiahaʻo Church today. (Credit: Mark Miller; Wikimedia Commons)

Hawaii: Industry Born

Another important aspect that signaled the end of ancient Hawaii was the introduction of the sugar industry. Sugarcane had been grown in Hawaii since around 600 CE. James Cook made a note of it when he arrived on the islands in 1778. As more traders, travelers, and missionaries came to Hawaii, sugar began to take a more important role. By the end of the 1800s, the sugar industry was one of the biggest, if not the biggest, industries on the islands. Over 337,000 people would make their way to Hawaii between the end of the 18th century to the end of the 19th century to take part in this booming industry.

With this in mind, the United States had a major interest in Hawaii and what it could produce, which included pineapples and coffee. For instance, in the 1960s, Hawaii produced 80 percent of the world's pineapple.

But we are jumping too far ahead with that. Let us take a look at how it all started. In 1802, the first sugar mill was established on Lāna'i, a small island in the center of the archipelago, just south of Moloka'i and Maui. This was actually constructed by a Chinese man, not a European or an American. Unfortunately, his name has been lost to history.

Soon, though, the first sugar plantation would be established by an American company. This was the Old Sugar Mill, and it came into being in 1835. The Native Hawaiians were not excited about this business taking up much of their land, but eventually, they relented. King Kamehameha III lent almost one thousand acres to the company, but initially, only twelve acres were planted.

The people running the Old Sugar Mill noted that the Hawaiians were "lazy." This, as you should know by now, was not true. Their culture was different from the capitalistic ethic that was spreading around the world at that time. The manager of the mill even went as far as to say that ten white men could produce the same amount of work as four hundred Hawaiians.

Workers were paid with money that could only be spent at the mill's stores, which means they were dependent on the Old Sugar Mill for practically everything. Eventually, the Hawaiians became frustrated enough that they decided to revolt. This, on top of the perceived lack of laziness, led to the Old Sugar Mill looking for workers from outside nations.

In 1844, the Old Sugar Mill closed down. But nevertheless, sugar plantations became an important part of Hawaii's economy during this decade. There was a ton of money to be made if you were able to grow and sell it, and over the century, sugar became one of the most valuable resources on a global scale. However, there was a problem. Sugar was not easy to produce.

Sugarcane is incredibly intensive to grow and tends to tire out the ground it grows in, meaning you cannot just keep planting crops on the same piece of land over and over again. To keep up with demand, more access to land was needed. What is more, sugarcane requires a lot of manpower to grow, nurture, and harvest, especially with the absence of machines back in the day.

This made Hawaii a prime location for the sugar industry. There were thousands of square miles of natural, incredibly fertile land available to be used for such a purpose, and there was an entire labor force of natives if necessary. These plantations established similar practices as the Old Sugar Mill, which kept the Native Hawaiians dependent on the sugar industry's growth.

The Native Hawaiian population numbers had been devastated due to the diseases brought to the islands, which means as the sugar industry continued to grow, foreigners came to the islands for opportunities, bringing more diseases. The demographics of the population were starting to change. Anglo-Americans were on the rise, although they never became the majority group. That honor belonged to Asians, who were imported or moved to the islands to work on sugarcane and pineapple plantations.

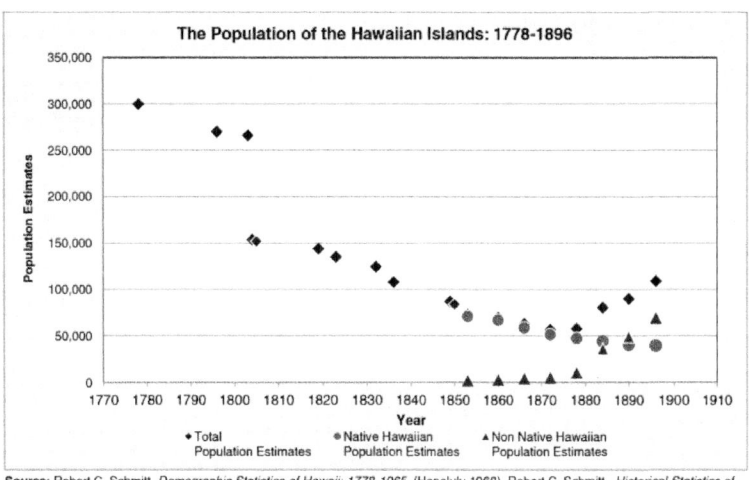

A graph of the population estimates of Hawaii.

Come the 1840s, sugar plantations practically dominated the Hawaiian agricultural landscape on every major island. Due to the introduction of steam-powered ships, shipping between the islands and importing and exporting products with other nations, namely the United States, became reliable and rapid. This was also fueled by the riches that were accumulated during the California gold rush, which was happening around this time period.

With businesses being heavily funded and the march of progress pretty much happening before many Native Hawaiians even knew what was happening, there was little they could do to stop what was happening. After all, this was not something that the Hawaiians had faced before.

Even King Kamehameha III was unaware of the consequences. Of course, the missionaries and plantation owners were paying money to rent the land from Kamehameha III, but they were seeking ways to obtain these lands for themselves. And eventually, they would succeed.

The End of the Era

Although ancient Hawaii ended with the formation of the Kingdom of Hawaii, it is important to realize just how much life on the islands would change within only a century. As you can see, the old way of doing things was pretty much over, as Western ideals had begun to creep onto the islands.

From the 1840s onward, the sugar and pineapple industries boomed, and the land across the archipelago became increasingly disputed. That is not to say that the Native Hawaiians, specifically the monarchy, did not try to stop it. In an attempt to keep up with modern times, the *ali'i*, which included the coveted Kamehameha bloodline, set up laws and processes to help Hawaiians take ownership of what was rightfully theirs.

For example, the Great Māhele introduced the concept of private property. However, Kamehameha wanted the Hawaiians to claim the land that was theirs. The land was divided into thirds, with one third going to the monarch, another third going to the *ali'i*, and the final third going to the common people. However, many Hawaiians were confused by the concept. The land was already theirs; why would they need to make an official claim on it? Few common Hawaiians made claims. These lands were eventually put up for sale, and most of the land went to businesses from the United States. It is believed that these businesses owned around 32 percent of Hawaii's lands.

Little by little, piece by piece, through changes in the law and monarchy, the Americans were able to take away ownership of the land. In 1898, just at the turn of the 20th century, Hawaii was annexed by President William McKinley. Hawaii would become a state of the United States in 1959.

Of course, this is putting it very simply. There was a lot of controversy behind what happened with Hawaii's annexation, such as a rebellion against the monarchy led by the United States. There were protests and coups. Queen Lili'uokalani (r. 1891-1893) and other *aliʻi* were arrested. The Kingdom of Hawaii was overthrown. If any of this interests you, we encourage you to read more about the history of Hawaii to gain a better understanding of what happened to the islands and how the Native Hawaiians are embracing their culture today. But our journey of ancient Hawaii has come to an end.

Conclusion

With the annexation of Hawaii complete, the Hawaiian archipelago was officially changed forever. Under the guidance of the United States government, Hawaii kept pace with the rest of the modern world and is home to many of the same ways of life as the Western mainland.

To some, it is a shame that colonialism and industrial efforts took Hawaii and transformed it into yet another aspect of their way of life. As you can tell from its history, Hawaii's ancient history is one of interest and deserves to be studied.

The Polynesians once sailed thousands of miles to discover the islands of Hawaii, where they created a thriving civilization. They lived off the land and learned how to work together to create a society that lived in balance with nature. It was more efficient and progressive in some ways than other societies at the time.

Of course, that does not mean that Hawaii's history did not have its fair share of violence and bloodshed. It surely did, and there is no doubt that Hawaii was the battleground for some of the most legendary conflicts and revolutions in history, especially for such a condensed population.

Nevertheless, it is a history that will never be forgotten any time soon, and if you were to travel to Hawaii today, you would see endless references, memorials, landmarks, museums, statues, artwork, and dedications to their ancient way of life. Hawaii's history is celebrated and revered, not just by the Hawaiian people of today but also throughout the world.

Travel to any of the islands today, and you will still find remnants of the old world. Temple structures, sacred symbols, parks, and tributes are everywhere. There has been a resurgence of the traditional way of life in recent years, and the Native Hawaiian population is making a comeback, although their numbers are still much lower than they should be. Regardless, their history should never be forgotten.

We remember their faith in their gods and their deep-rooted rituals. We celebrate their master crafting skills and their resilience and dedication to maintaining their traditions. There should be little doubt in your mind that one of the most inspirational cultures to have ever lived was the Hawaiians. And their land and people uphold a legacy that will last forever.

Part 2: History of Hawaii

A Captivating Guide to Hawaiian History

Introduction

This book contains a curated walkthrough of the history of Hawai'i from the very beginnings of its ancient seafaring ways to the modern incarnation of the US state. Much has happened within this timeframe, and the adventures of Hawai'i's people, legends, and culture are a sight to behold. Explanations have been included wherever pertinent, and a reader should have no problem using this book as a starting point to dive into the rich history of this region.

This book traces a path through Hawai'i's ideology and religious thoughts, which is unique but also severely underrepresented in mainstream media depictions of the region. This book also chronicles the rise of the Hawaiian kings of old, which occurred both as a natural response to maintain order and as part of the evolution to make contact with the outside world. For many reasons, Hawai'i had long been isolated from the emerging cultures and superpowers of the world, and now its footsteps through time are being illuminated. Hawai'i had a tumultuous role to play during the Second World War, with a pivotal event occurring on its soil. However, as you will learn in this book, this event did not occur out of the blue. Within these chapters lies the story of the slow and inevitable build-up of tensions and competing national interests that ultimately resulted in "a day that will live in infamy."

Even after such an event, Hawaiʻi managed to move on, heal, and synthesize an identity that literally and figuratively draws from both ends of the Pacific Ocean and from within the islands themselves to forge a modern state that has gifted the world with brilliant people. In fact, some of them are featured in this book. There will be a detailed look into their lives and accomplishments, which are, for the most part, set against the backdrop of Hawaiʻi. Additionally, this book offers a truer sense of what is behind the things we take as "quintessentially" Hawaiian and also takes a look into some of the challenges of modern Hawaiʻi.

Jump in, and become immersed in a world of lore, tragedy, and, ultimately, triumph. This world of inspiring tales and strange facts has somehow escaped widespread attention and coverage, but that is no longer the case. With this book, readers hold the key to pierce through the mystique and tropical mythos of Hawaiʻi and unveil the truth.

Chapter 1 – Introductory Overview

No single book can cover the entire breadth and depth of the storied records of Hawai'i. The region is so surprisingly rich that in its comparatively short existence of a thousand or so years, multiple shelves full of books would not be enough to describe all that is noteworthy of Hawai'i. Thus, this book is meant to serve not just as an overview but also as a selection of events and times in Hawai'i's history that are particularly salient, relevant, representative, and well-documented. Great care and attention have been paid to the sources used within this work, along with the portrayal of the region's history. We hope that the book serves as a deeply engaging and refreshing first dive into the history of Hawai'i.

To understand the history of Hawai'i, one must first be able to picture it geographically. Humanity and the actions of men and women are what usually form the bulk of history, but the location, topography, and climate of Hawai'i are not only unique aspects of the state but also critically important factors in its history. Hawai'i is located at the eastern end of Oceania, a sub-region that can be divided into Micronesia, a region of islands located north of New Guinea and east of the Philippines; Melanesia, a region including

New Guinea and extending to the east and south of it; and Polynesia, a large, triangular region that is even farther east of Melanesia, with two of its tips extending into the Northern and Southern Hemispheres.

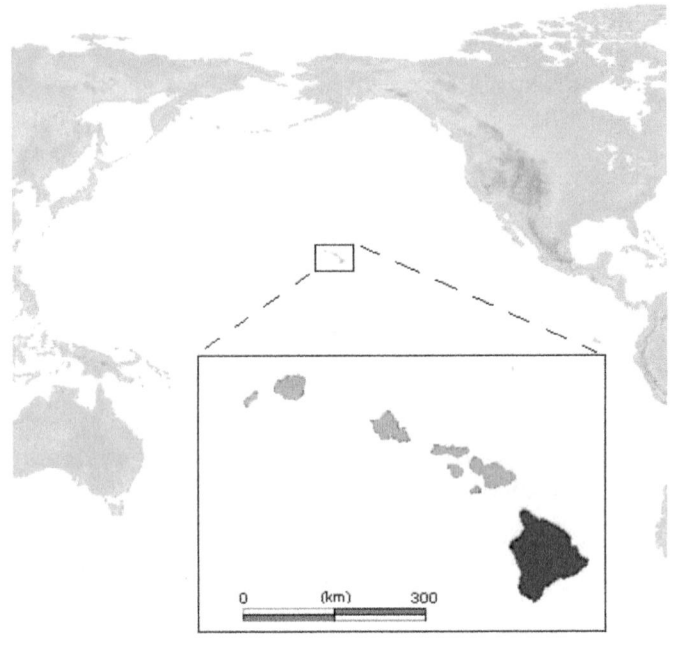

The location of the Hawaiian Islands relative to the Americas on the right and Asia and Australia on the left. (Source: Wikimedia Commons, M. Minderhoud)

At the northern tip of the Polynesian Triangle lies Hawai'i, and even though Hawai'i is nowadays a part of the United States of America, it is the only state that lies outside of North America (although politically it is a part of it). At the other end of the Polynesian Triangle lies New Zealand and Easter Island. Additionally, the State of Hawaii is not a single landmass but rather a group of islands called an archipelago. Hawai'i consists of over one hundred islands, many of which are too small to be properly classified as islands. For most intents and purposes, Hawai'i consists of eight major islands: the island called Hawai'i itself, Maui, O'ahu, Kaua'i, Moloka'i, Lana'i, Ni'ihau, and Kaho'olawe.

Together, these eight islands make up more than 90 percent of the emergent land area of the Hawaiian archipelago.

These islands lie about 20 degrees north of the equator in latitude and about 157 degrees west of Greenwich in longitude. This means that Hawaiʻi experiences a stable and predictable season. Later, we will see how these ideal conditions for agriculture helped steer Hawaiʻi's history. Their position shows little deviation in seasonal day length as well. This is due to Hawaiʻi being relatively close to the equator, which means it is not as affected by the sun's yearly north-to-south shift between the tropics of Cancer and Capricorn. The longest summer day in Hawaiʻi is just over thirteen hours long, and the shortest day is a little under eleven hours long, a minor difference.

Hawaiʻi, the largest island, bearing the same name as the state itself, has the nickname "the Big Island," and it has a population of around 200,000 people. Maui, the second-largest island, is more than five times smaller than the Big Island, and most of the other islands are comparable in size to Maui. The island of Oʻahu, known as "the Gathering Place," actually has the highest population of the eight major islands, with over 900,000 people inhabiting it. Kauaʻi is known as "the Garden Isle" due to its extremely fertile lands and history of sugar plantations.

The Hawaiian Islands are home to some of the highest mountains in the world, with Mauna Loa and Mauna Kea rivaling mountains from the Alps. Both are well over four thousand meters (over thirteen thousand feet) high. Although Mauna Kea is now considered a dormant volcano, Mauna Loa is not. In fact, it is still under constant monitoring and surveillance, as it has the potential for hazardous eruptions and is located near populated areas. However, most of Hawaiʻi's eruptions and volcanic activity aren't overtly dangerous to human or animal life, as its lava flows are usually slow. Due to Hawaiʻi's isolation from other countries and cities, as well as the sheer height of these two mountains, they are some of the best locations for solar and astronomical observatories.

A panoramic view of the Mauna Kea observatories. (Source: Wikimedia Commons, Frank Ravizza)

Hawai'i is quite isolated, as it is located near the middle of the Pacific Ocean, far from any major landmasses. This also means that it was far removed from any major centers of civilization, resulting in a culture and people that are truly unique. It has mountainous areas and volcanic activity due to its geological hotspot, which is a unique geological phenomenon due to Hawai'i being located far from the edges of its tectonic plate. Most volcanoes occur when tectonic plates diverge away from each other or crush together.

Due to its central location in the Pacific Ocean, Hawai'i lies sandwiched between the United States of America and Japan, two powerful nations that have played major roles in charting

Hawai'i's course through history. And although this seems like the reason why Captain James Cook, a British explorer and captain in the Royal Navy, eventually named the Hawaiian Islands the "Sandwich Islands," it isn't the real reason. Captain Cook was the first European to document and popularize the trip to the Hawaiian Islands, and he named them in honor of his patron, the Earl of Sandwich, who happened to be the First Lord of the British Admiralty at the time.

The view of Mauna Loa (right) and Mauna Kea (left), as seen and depicted in the 1820s. (Source: Hiram Bingham, A Residence of Twenty-one Years in the Sandwich Islands, *1849)*

Located north of the equator, Hawai'i is a tropical region, and it maintains a windy and warm climate year-round. Only the tallest mountain areas experience any snowfall, and most of Hawai'i cycles through a wet season and dry season.

Much of Hawai'i's history is influenced by its tropical climate, which allowed for rich agricultural exports and industries. These agricultural revolutions would forever change both the political and ethnic makeup of the islands, attracting global political scrutiny and tens of thousands of migrant labor workers. Later on, these agricultural exports would also go on to shape the world's perception of what "Hawaiian cuisine" was, often erroneously. Interestingly, the surface of the islands of Hawai'i contains an immense range of distinctive features. Hawai'i boasts both windswept, flat beaches and windy, rocky crags. The southern and southeastern slopes of Mauna Loa and Kilauea, two of Hawai'i's active volcanoes, have several long lines of cliffs. These were formed early on when huge portions of the growing mountains slumped into the ocean, either incrementally or suddenly. These ancient, massive landslides sent silt, rock, and volcanic debris tumbling out over the ocean floor for over one hundred miles.

These great landslides continue into the present day, with the most recent one occurring in 1975, which triggered an earthquake.

The Hawaiian Islands have both desolate plains of igneous rock and dense, humid rainforests. These mature forests undoubtedly began when algae, lichen, mosses, and ferns began growing on the cooled surface of volcanic basalt and ash. Over time, the weathered rocks and surfaces of the islands would mix with organic material, giving rise to true soil and allowing later stages of floral growth to take root. Hawaiian tarweeds, *Pukiawe*, Hawaiian blueberries, and red tree ferns are just some examples of the many species of vegetation that inhabit the Hawaiian Islands. Hawaiian rainforests also harbor species like *Acacia koa* and *Cheirodendron* (also known as *'olapa*). Hawaiian rainforests are also graded or zoned, mostly according to elevation and other climatic factors. The temperature decreases as the elevation increases, giving rise to floral variation and different kinds of forests. Lowland rainforests are below the mountain rainforests, and both are located below an altitude of 2,000 meters (6,500 feet). This is followed by cool, dry forests and alpine scrub at the higher peaks of Maui and Hawai'i.

These differing climates are due partly to the trade winds that constantly blow against Hawai'i and also partly to the mountainous topography of the islands. These two forces have an interplay between them that allow moisture, rains, storms, and temperatures to fluctuate and stagnate, depending on the location. Notably, the trade winds that come from the east flow over mountains, hills, and valleys to produce drafts and gusts almost all over the islands. A lot of the ocean is cooled by a return current of cold water that runs down from the region of the Bering Straits. Taken together, these mean that the Hawaiian Islands are several degrees cooler than any other island at roughly the same latitude. On the whole, though, Hawai'i's east-facing and west-facing sides are noticeably different. Its eastern sides are windy, rainy, and heavily wooded, with thick forests. The western sides are much sparser in vegetation, being warmer and drier. This difference in plant life is obvious enough to be seen from true color satellite images of Hawai'i.

Hawai'i has a hurricane season that runs from June to November, but the group of islands is buttressed from any real threat by the cooler waters that surround them. Nonetheless, tropical storms are frequent and bring lots of rain, modest winds, and occasionally some property damage.

Significant amounts of metal are rare on the Hawaiian Islands, which meant that Native Hawaiians have had to be very resourceful and creative in finding and utilizing new materials to work with. Most of the major forms of fauna that inhabit the Hawaiian Islands were introduced by the first settlers of the island, who came from New Guinea and parts of Southeast Asia. These animals include dogs, rats, pigs, chickens, and other types of fowl. Notably, of the five species of marine turtles that are found in the central region of the Pacific Ocean, two of them regularly nest on the Hawaiian Islands. One of them is the green sea turtle, or *honu*, and they regularly nest at the smaller, uninhabited northwestern islands of the Hawaiian archipelago. Sometimes, they lay eggs and nest on Moloka'i and even, at least historically, on the island of Lana'i. The other turtle, the hawksbill turtle, or *honu'ea* or simply *ea*, is much less commonly sighted. In the past, its thick shell, which is patterned in an attractive way, was a valuable material to manufacture ornaments from.

For a nation so geographically isolated, Hawai'i is one of the most recognizable and influential island nations in the world, and its deep and diverse history reflects this.

Chapter 2 – Ancient Hawai'i: The People of Hawai'i

Sadly, the earlier histories of Hawai'i are not well documented and have been somewhat eroded due to contact with the outside world. However, lots of evidence, archaeological clues, and connections with the surrounding cultures, peoples, and islands paint a picture that allows us to learn much about the people of ancient Hawai'i.

Origins

Although the exact date of human colonization of the islands of Hawai'i is not accurately known, most scholars and experts on the subject agree that the Polynesian people first set foot on Hawai'i around 900 to 1,100 years ago (around 1100 CE). Prehistoric Polynesians and, by extension, Hawaiians descend from the people of the Lapita culture, named after an archaeological site in New Caledonia (located in the South Pacific). The Lapita people, in turn, seem to have descended from regions of Southeast Asia. Since they are so ancient, one of their more well-known cultural artifacts is a particular type of pottery that has come to be known as Lapita ware, with stamped designs and patterns ringing their bowls and pots. It is very likely that the Lapita people had the hallmarks of many Polynesian peoples. They most likely had adept seafaring skills, utilized various marine resources to the fullest, and had a habit of bringing along animal and plant life, which helped sustain them on new islands.

These ancient Austronesians were skilled sailors, navigators, and explorers, discovering islands to the north, south, and east of modern-day New Guinea and Australia. They progressively moved from one island cluster to another, colonizing inhabitable lands and venturing far out into the Pacific Ocean.

Specifically, the Lapita people spread outward and eastward from the Bismarck Archipelago, located off the northeastern coast of New Guinea, reaching parts of Melanesia around 1250 BCE. Most of their settlements ran along the shores of newly discovered islands, notably not encroaching any great distance farther inland. This prevented them from interacting significantly with any indigenous occupants that might have already populated some of the islands and lands. On the Solomon Islands and some parts of the Bismarck Archipelago, stilt houses were built on the rockier beaches and reef areas.

It is theorized that the Lapita people had an extensive trading network amongst their previous settlements, even though the distance between them would have been quite far. Invariably, the Lapita people would have traded goods and products, which were often sourced from the sea, for other materials and products from people that lived farther upland and inland. This, along with the Lapita people's inhabitance of only coastal areas, would have made them desirable allies and friends. They would have been useful and reliable in providing raw marine resources and other things not available to land-locked communities.

A piece of Lapita pottery found at the Bourewa site in Fiji, approximately three thousand years old. (Source: Wikimedia Commons, Patrick Nunn)

Not stopping at Melanesia, the Lapita culture spread out toward the Fiji Islands and even Tonga and Samoa, which lay farther east. This period, approximately around 1000 BCE, marks the oldest estimate of possible incursions into Polynesia. Subtle changes to the shape and designs of the Lapita pottery are able to be progressively tracked and dated, allowing archaeologists to discern their probable movements eastward into Polynesia. Additionally, since these ancient seafarers brought both plants and animals with them to settle onto new islands, modern historians have another angle they can use to track their migration patterns.

The earliest reliable archaeological, linguistic, and animal DNA evidence suggests that Hawai'i was discovered and settled from the Marquesas Islands, which lie a little over 3,000 kilometers (1,860 miles) to the southeast of Hawai'i, around 600 CE. Hawai'i also had a significant Tahitian influence due to multiple visits to and from the Society Islands, of which Tahiti is a part. These visits and interactions occurred around 1100 CE. In fact, the channel of water that runs from the Hawaiian island of Maui southward that passes between Lanaʻi and Kahoʻolawe is called Kealaikahiki, which literally translates to "the path to Tahiti."

Masters of the Ocean

At some point in time, ancient Austronesian people invented the outrigger canoe, a boat with a single hull that was lashed to smaller wings on either side for added stability, storage, and buoyancy. The exact progression of their inventions and innovations are not known, but there is solid evidence of different forms of these canoes, with some even being fitted with sails for longer journeys. It is also very probable that the peoples of the Lapita culture and the subsequent Polynesians developed the double-hulled canoe and used it for journeys that were hundreds of kilometers long.

Outrigger canoes at Waikiki Beach, circa late 1800s. (Source: Hawaiʻi State Archives)

Specifically, ancient Hawaiians used the great endemic Koa trees (*Acacia koa*) to fashion hulls over fifty feet long from a single trunk. They also made other technological advances, such as plating for their wooden hulls, innovations in sail rigging, caulking, and lashing, among other things. These progressive improvements meant that their ships, though wooden, were extremely seaworthy. These large crafts could carry several families, their supplies, domestic animals, and plants to spread on any newly discovered island.

All evidence points to them using celestial navigation and being skilled sailors, repairmen, divers, fishermen, and swimmers. Archaeological and oral traditions tell us that early Hawaiians took their time to perfect and improve their ships and sailing routes. They planned ahead and prepared supplies for long voyages while employing concepts of zenith stars, fixed stars, and seasonal winds for navigation and travel.

The journeys made by ancient Hawaiians and Polynesians were so unbelievably far and dangerous that many anthropologists did not believe the archaeological and linguistic similarities and evidence. In essence, they were convinced that the navigation and technology possessed by the Native Hawaiians were not sufficiently advanced to allow for such journeys. Crossing from the Northern to the Southern Hemisphere also meant that certain celestial navigation tools and techniques would have to be adjusted accordingly and on the fly. This uncertainty stayed ingrained in academic writing and the general consensus for decades.

It was only until Ben Rudolph Finney met Mau Piailug that the debate was truly settled. Ben Finney was an American anthropologist who specialized in surfing, sailing, and navigation. He, along with Herbert Kawainui Kane and Charles Tommy Holmes, founded the Polynesian Voyaging Society, a research and educational society. Mau Piailug was a Micronesian wayfinder who was an expert in non-instrument navigation and open-ocean voyaging, skills that were acquired through rote learning and memorizing the oral traditions of his people. Together with a crew consisting of mostly Native Hawaiians, Finney and Piailug bravely set out on an expedition in 1976, starting from the Hawaiian Islands toward the Society Islands. The ship they used was a double-hulled canoe named *Hokuleʻa*, which was constructed in a traditional Polynesian design, and they sailed and navigated using only ancient methods. After a month-long voyage, they successfully reached the Society Islands and proved the trip was perfectly possible without the use of modern equipment or navigational methods.

The deck and fabric-sheltered sleeping area of the Hokule'a, *the double-hulled canoe used to sail from Hawai'i to Tahiti. (Source: Wikimedia Commons, Tonitt)*

Ancient Hawaiians also knew the tides well, correlating them with lunar events and a semidiurnal schedule. Similarly, the occurrence of tsunamis is also posited to be a regular occurrence in prehistoric Hawai'i. About every four to five years, a noticeable tsunami would reach the Hawaiian Islands, making a dent in the oral histories and memories of ancient Hawaiians. They would then have stayed away from shores that were prone to tsunami swells, areas like the northeastern coast of Hawai'i. Even in recent years, tsunami waves ten meters (thirty-three feet) tall heavily damaged the urban areas of Hawai'i. Today, early detection and warning systems are in place to help prevent loss of life and damage.

Food, Flora, and Fauna

The mainstay of ancient Polynesian and Hawaiian diets consisted of starch-rich tubers like the taro plant (*Colocasia esculenta*) and the purple yam or greater yam (*Dioscorea alata*). Both plants feature prominently in social etiquette, mythology, and rituals. These plants, along with marine animals, formed the main pillars of Native Hawaiian cuisine.

A Hawaiian man transporting harvested taro plants, circa 1898. (Source: Vue 21. Recueil. Îles Hawaï. IV. Culture. Documents iconographiques, compiled by Louis Pierre Vossion)

The Kuroshio Current, which runs from the Philippines and the southern Japanese islands, combines with the North Pacific Current to bring most of Hawai'i's marine animals to its archipelago. A similar situation plays out on the southern groups of islands in the Pacific Ocean. Additionally, other marine species would have "island-hopped" their way westward, eventually reaching the Hawaiian archipelago. The coasts of Hawai'i are rich with many different species of seaweeds, corals, mollusks, and bony fish. In all except certain parts of the youngest Hawaiian Islands, living coral reefs surround the coasts of the islands and extend far out into the ocean, becoming more of a "coral-algal" zone farther out. Calling Hawai'i an oasis in the middle of the Pacific Ocean is not an inaccurate statement.

Hawai'i's fish, however, mostly come from the Indo-West Pacific, showing little to no contribution from the eastern side of the Pacific Ocean (the side of the Americas). This is due to much colder currents and an extensive deep-water gap between Hawai'i and the American continents. Some specific examples of Hawai'i's fish are the saddle wrasse or *hinalea lau-wili*, the milletseed butterflyfish or *lau wiliwili*, and the lined coris or *malamalama*. Other nonspecific fish include different types of moray eels, scorpionfishes, groupers, surgeonfishes, jacks, and parrotfishes.

Some of the vitally important plants that were frequently brought over to other islands were the paper mulberry tree, also known as the *tapa* cloth tree (*Broussonetia papyrifera*), the coconut tree, and the palm lily or *ki* tree. The paper mulberry, in particular, was cultivated for its inner bark, which was slowly peeled, soaked, and then beaten to manufacture barkcloth, or *kapa*. Barkcloth was used not only for clothing and decorative purposes but also as tapestries and a form of canvas that was painted on.

An artist's depiction of a Hawaiian woman pounding natural fibers to make the clothes they use to dress themselves, 1819. (Source: Wikimedia Commons, Hiart. Original work by Jacques Etienne Victor Arago, Honolulu Museum of Art)

Coconut plants would have multiple uses, from building timber to starting fires to creating ropes, which were spun from its fibers. The nutritional content of the coconut also meant that most ancient Polynesians treasured the coconut tree for all its uses, earning it the nickname of "the tree of life." Other plants that ancient Polynesians and Hawaiians would bring along with them included bananas, breadfruit, and Polynesian arrowroot.

Ancient Life

Ancient Hawaiians almost definitely had an agrarian lifestyle and possessed a complex, communal society that included caste systems. The highest rung consisted of chiefs and leaders of villages and regions. Priests, shamans, healers, and professional craftsmen made up the majority of the second rung of the caste system, followed by the common people who made up most of the population. It is also very likely that even in ancient Hawai'i, society was organized around the concept of an extended family unit, the *ohana*. This unit was very important to ancient Hawaiians because it was connected to their caste system, the ruling class, genealogical naming of family gods, and even the ownership of land. Further kinship groups would develop from the *ohana*, and aggregations of these would then form villages or inhabit a region. The overall task of the *ohana* was to cultivate, find, hunt, or harvest food and other raw materials, whether from agricultural or marine sources. These would be used to sustain both the *ohana* and the larger group that it belonged to, along with other requirements of trading, levies, religious offerings, and more.

Although ancient Hawaiian agriculture was not as advanced as other mass-producing agricultural civilizations, it was nonetheless systematic and reliable enough to not only maintain an adequate supply of food but also to grow the population at a steady rate. Such a feat was accomplished not with metal tools or animal-driven implements but rather with a system of work allocation and group effort. There is also evidence of more advanced agricultural constructions and aquaculture practices dating back to the ancient Hawaiians. Freshwater ponds and multilevel terraces were constructed to help crops like taro and sweet potato to grow and flourish.

Meat from swine and fowl would serve only as supplementary food sources and not as the main staples of everyday life. Hunting would very likely be carried out simultaneously alongside gathering, with the activity being one that involved the entire family. Similarly, fishing and marine resource collection was a family affair, especially in the shallower coastal areas. Deepsea fishing would only be done by specialists, as they had to employ large canoes, deep-sea fishing lines, spears, nets, and expert diving and swimming techniques. Old records of oral histories of ancient Hawai'i tell of fleets of canoes going out to sea with many men in a massive effort to catch fish and other marine life. The people would prepare in advance for such expeditions, preparing long braided fishing lines and different types of hooks and spears. Some of the largest nets would hold enough fish that they needed ten to twenty canoes to help bring the catch back to shore.

A manuscript sketch of Hawaiian natives with their animals by Louis Choris, a GermanRussian painter and explorer who was known for his expedition research sketching.

Margaret Titcomb, an American librarian who wrote several books on Hawai'i, claims that the dog in the center of the painting is the only depiction of the now-extinct Hawaiian poi dog. (Source: Honolulu Academy of Arts, original work by Louis Choris, 1816) Canoes were critically important in helping secure bountiful harvests of marine protein. These ships would also be used for trading, exploration, settlement of new areas, and religious rituals.

Thus, canoe-making in ancient Hawai'i was a revered and specialized craft. It is known that canoe-making was held in high regard in pre-European Hawai'i, complete with all the attendant concepts and practices of strict apprenticeship and deep mastery, which took years. The work was surrounded by the appropriate ceremonies and rituals that were performed by priests and shamans, from the mere selection of which log was to be felled to the dragging of the finished vessel down to the water.

One of the most alien concepts to Native Hawaiians was that one could possess sources of water like lakes and rivers and the right to their use. Early Hawaiians regarded water as utterly inseparable from the land itself, believing that bodies of water were communally owned. Such an attitude toward the sanctity of water would help explain how large irrigation projects and manmade water streams on the Hawaiian Islands came about, as the amount of labor needed was immense and could only be accomplished through a concerted, collective effort. Writings from old Native Hawaiian farmers state that "Water, then, like sunlight, as a source of life to land and man, was the possession of no man, not even the *ali'i nui* [chiefs] or the *mo'i* [ruler]."

Kings, Rulers, and Commoners

The kinship politics of ancient Hawai'i were headed by high chiefs called *ali'i*. These chiefs would rule over districts of an island along with their families. Leaders that were secondary to the *ali'i* were called *konohiki* and were responsible for overseeing and stewarding the *ahupua'a*. The *ahupua'a* is a section of land on the island that took into consideration access to water, fertile ground, residential areas, high ground, and many other factors in its allotment to a family or group. One way to conceptualize the *ahupua'a* is to visualize a "weirdly-shaped pizza slice" of land from an island that made sure to include all the needs of an *ohana* or village. The *konohiki* were usually distant relatives of the high chiefs and also helped them govern the common people, or *maka'ainana*. Even amongst the *maka'ainana*, there were societal classes and hierarchical divisions.

High chiefs of large districts or even entire islands would be met with respect and prostration; any sign of blatant disrespect was punishable by death. A ruler's clothes could not be worn by common men, and his house was a sacred place where only those who were permitted could enter. A high chief would be attended to and advised by a group of nobles, which traditionally favored the paternal side of the family. Some of the lesser-ranked members of the king's cohort would be responsible for waiting on him, helping him stay cool with fans, bathing and massaging him, and fetching him food and drinks. Other members would be treasurers, heralds, runners, and chief stewards that would report daily activities to the king. Furthermore, the court would consist of storytellers, dancers, musicians, guards, diviners, priests, and wayfinders.

Skilled craftsmen like canoe-makers, healers, and rope and net makers would be ranked the highest amongst the common people, followed by the farmers, workers, and their family members (they made up the largest group of the population). Religious leaders and priests would be individuals held in high esteem regardless of the caste system, as they served the gods and helped bridge the gap between what was man and what was divine. The duties and responsibilities held by the priests were vast. They would hold ceremonies to appease the gods of land and water for agricultural success. They would read signs and advise rulers on auspicious times for harvesting, fishing, sailing, and exploring. They would also help ward off calamitous storms, volcanic activity, disease, and tsunamis. These priests, shamans, and sorcerers were collectively known as *kahuna*. Lastly, as is common with many other civilizations, prisoners of war and criminals were at the bottom of the social ladder, and they were called *kauwa*.

Amongst the commoners, there are two prevailing theories of exactly what the *ohana* included and meant. The first theory speculates that *ohana* referred to all the families that were living in that area. Such a grouping of families would occupy an *ili*, which was a subdivision of the *ahupua'a*. The *ili* would include dry land, wet land, and inhabitable land. The *ohana* living here would pay their taxes to their group's leader, and the amount was calculated in proportion to the land allotted.

Such taxes would invariably contribute to the royal tax, which proceeded in a pyramidal manner upward. The royal tax was mostly made up of articles of food, so there would be bundles of fruit, taro, and sweet potato along with portions of meat from dogs, hogs, fowl, and fish. Other gifts could be precious stones, beautiful shells, rare bird feathers, and polished rock decorations and jewelry. Still, a separate labor tax would also be enacted upon the *maka'ainana*. Some of them would be tasked to tend to the gardens that belonged to the royal family, and others would be sent out for public work like repairing and building temples, advancing irrigation projects, and constructing new houses. Justice would have probably taken the form of a complaint system to family heads, then to the *konohiki*, and perhaps even to the king himself. Legal proceedings wouldn't be much more than sentencing, and petty crimes would see private revenge. More serious crimes were punished by execution, which was carried out by the chiefs' *ila'muku*, or executioner. This ensured a decent level of serious crime deterrence.

The second theory of what *ohana* meant in ancient Hawai'i is that it was not a genealogically driven concept but merely a kindred network. This relaxed definition of a family meant that a group system of cooperation was prioritized and also allowed for shifting access to the land as needs arose. This theory is further supported by the fact that maintaining genealogical lines among the commoners was forbidden by the *ali'i*. Allowing inheritances and rigid notions of the family to take root would have led, and indeed did lead to, conflict and wars.

TATTOOED HAWAIIAN CHIEF, DRAWN BY JACQUES ARAGO,
ARTIST WITH FREYCINET.

A depiction of a chief or officer of King Kamehameha II in full traditional dress, circa 1819. (Source: Iles Sandwich, un Officier du Roi en Grand Costume, Jacques Arago and Freycinet)

Early on in Hawai'i's development, blood ties would have been the main factor in determining *ohana*. In time, however, only high chiefs and rulers would be allowed genealogical titles of great importance, making marriage within their own families a frequent practice. As time went on, power would be determined by marriages and warfare. Commoners would have little to no property rights that were linked to bloodlines and family possession. The *maka'ainana* would be moved about by war and conquest, maintaining loose ties to extended families. The redistribution of land and reallocation of land stewardship, which would happen after new bouts of conquest, unavoidably shifted these groups around. Defeated rulers would sometimes lose their societal standing and become commoners themselves, but being offered as a sacrifice to the gods was also common for conquered rulers. Sometimes they would even become or choose to become social outcasts or untouchables (*kauwa*).

Although there seems to be little evidence of a distinct warrior class, specially trained military guards were dispatched to guard royalty and lead invasions or defenses against intruders. Most of the people of ancient Hawai'i were trained in the use of weapons and occasionally drilled in groups, where they engaged in mock fights and learned battle techniques. Ancient Hawaiian weapons were similar to the rest of the world, as they used spears, daggers, clubs, slings, and javelins. Notably, Hawaiians did not employ shields of any sort; instead, they resorted to becoming experts in avoiding, catching, and parrying thrown weapons coming at them. Bows and arrows were not widely used in warfare, as they were mostly only utilized in hunting and vermin extermination. Ambush tactics and fights on open fields were the prevailing strategies, but sea battles would sometimes see upward of a hundred canoes on each side clashing. Largescale sea fights were rare, though, due to the amount of preparation, manpower, and materials that were required.

Interestingly, Hawaiian mythology tells of different races of dwarf people, wild hunters, and forest dwellers who lived on the islands before the first people of Hawai'i ever reached land. These people are collectively called Menehune, but no concrete historical evidence of such people has been discovered. In other Central Polynesian islands, the older term *manahune* referred to slaves or workers of a lower social rank and status. It is quite likely that these practices were mostly abandoned in ancient Hawai'i but that the term stuck around. As the tales slowly morphed into legends, the aspect of low social status might have slowly changed over time to refer to the diminutive physical size of the Menehune.

Temples

The ancient people of Hawai'i built elaborate and large temples called *heiau*, many of which were unfortunately destroyed due to pressure from Christian missionaries and Western contact.

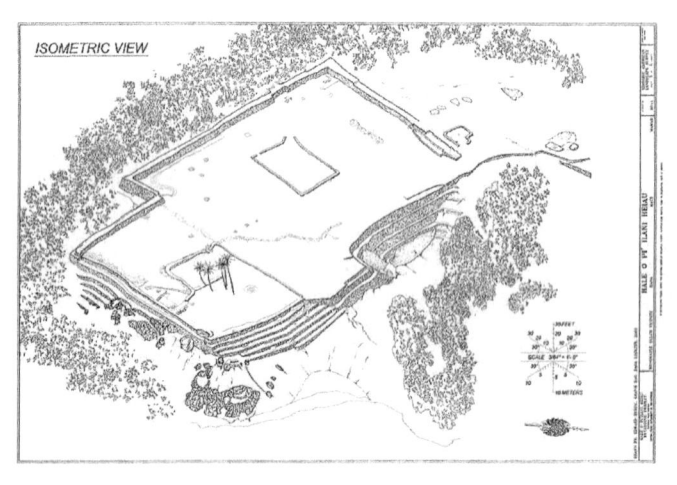

An overhead isometric view of the Hale O Pi'ilani Heiau, Maui. The image shows terraced borders and sectioned parts for different purposes and crowds. (Source: Historic American Landscapes Survey, Edward Byrdy, Khanh Dao, Dana Lockett)

Most *heiaus* were simple structures, but they were not meant to be works of art. Broken pieces of cooled lava were often found around the sites of older *heiaus*, and water-smoothened pebbles were worked into the mud and onto the floors to ensure a relatively smooth surface upon which to walk and kneel. Grass-thatched huts with massive stone and rock walls would be built on elevated parts of the ground or on terraced ground. Simplicity permeated the images of the gods, sometimes even bordering on the crude. *Heiau* sites were almost invariably walled around, whether in a rectangular layout or a circular one.

Still, some *heiaus* were deliberately elaborate, with the largest ones being many stories tall. They were built primarily with religious purposes in mind. *Heiaus* would be built to venerate the gods, influence the weather, and pray for success in agriculture and war. These structures were made from many different types of materials, including sand, lava rock, sandstone, and coral. In the course of worshiping their many gods, Hawaiians would serve up offerings of incense, fish, meats, sacred barkcloth, fruits, bounties of agricultural harvest, and, during certain times of war, human sacrifices. However, perhaps the most important part of worship was chanting prayers, with the most sacred of these rituals being chanted by a high priest. Scaffolding would be erected within the *heiau*. This structure was called *Lananu'umamao*, so named because the scaffolding was constructed in three stages: the *nu'u* (earth), *lani* (heavens), and *mamao* (a faraway place that was within hearing distance). The entire structure would be covered in white barkcloth, and only the more distinguished members of society could "ascend" into the inner parts of the *Lananu'umamao*. The last and most sacred stage could only be entered by the high priest and the ruling chief. Each step of this scaffolding would have prayers and offerings; it was, in essence, a stage-by-stage ritual that incorporated a series of prayers, images, and other objects, like bent saplings, cords, and drums.

Chapter 3 – Ancient Hawai'i: The Gods and Myths of Hawai'i

Ancient Hawaiians were polytheistic and animistic, with many of their mythological and theological beliefs bleeding into their approaches and ideology toward land ownership, societal norms, sailing practices, farming practices, and warfare. This divine nature was also intensely expressed in their notion of sovereignty, as kings and rulers were believed to be descended from the gods. It was thought they possessed a sacred and religious character. Superstitious awe and ritualistic proceedings would follow new royal births, as well as visits to holy sites, *heiaus*, and volcanic mountains. Legends and myths regularly reference and use lightning and thunder as heralds of an important event. This divine nature would be reflected in their red feather cloaks, helmets, and capes, and only those of royal blood would be permitted to don such clothing.

Firstly, it is important to understand that to capture Hawaiian mythology is to capture the entire range of storytelling that encapsulates folklore, oral traditions, superstitions, prayers, chants, and many other such things. Moreover, such a deep mythology, one that was spread over hundreds of years and over vast distances and different islands, needed to incorporate the culture, economy, and ideology of the ancient Hawaiian people.

Among Hawaiians and even more so for ancient Hawaiians, the usage of the word for god, *akua*, is not fixed and determinate. The word may refer to almost any object of nature, manmade image, or even phenomena of nature. In other words, the gods and mythology of ancient Hawai'i are intrinsically naturalistic and, to some extent, animistic. Another important philosophical concept among ancient Hawaiians is the relation of the individual to the physical universe around them through the use of pairing opposites. The ideas of night and day, light and darkness, male and female, or land and water permeate Hawaiian mythology and the composition of chants.

Gods are often represented in Hawaiian stories as chiefs and lords, and they sometimes dwelled in fantastical lands and abodes in the heavens. Of the great gods that are worshiped, none are mentioned more often than the gods Ku, Kane, Lono, and Kanaloa, as evidenced by multiple early missionary writings and letters. These gods are often invoked together in chants and songs. In fact, the first prayer of some ceremonies is often nothing more than an enumeration and invocation of the numerous names of the god or gods that are being worshiped through that ceremony.

Gods would also have families, so there would be subordinate gods within those families. These "lesser gods" would be invoked by those who hoped to gain something that was specifically associated with the lesser gods, such as certain skills or success in a particular activity. Even thieves had a patron god in Hawaiian mythology. It is probable that the four

"Great Gods" were first conceived of as nature deities with universal significance and powers, only to be associated with particular human beings and human traits later on. This would explain why some Native Hawaiians looked upon Captain James Cook as Lono because they thought the god had returned to them in the form of this impressive, albeit alien, man. In other words, divinity is thought of as lying dormant and being infused with normal, everyday things, such as water. It manifests itself in an obvious physical form only when active. This placed further importance on genealogical descent for ancient Hawaiians.

As is the case with many other cultures, Hawaiian mythology recognizes a period of history before humans when spirits and gods alone populated the seas and the lands. There is a noted absence of detailed primeval or cosmic mythology. Later migrations from Tahiti, which was once called "Kahiki," have also left their mark on chants and legends, which is evidenced by linguistic identities and corresponding forms, such as morphemes, phonologically similar names, etc. The Hawaiians kept their ancestral bonds with Kahiki alive, as they honored them as the progenitor of the family line. Plots of heroic tales and romances trace back to the chiefs in Tahiti.

Kahuna

Even the priests of ancient Hawai'i were divided into several orders, some of which were hereditary in nature. Rote memorization was highly emphasized as the method of teaching and communication, resulting in a special duty for priests. They had to commit to memory the long prayers and naming systems of gods and family gods. Hence, the *kahuna*, besides being the priests and shamans of the islands, were also the learned class of ancient Hawai'i, passing on the accumulated knowledge of astronomy, history, medicine, philosophy, and theology. Later on, the term would change to also encapsulate the meaning of "expert" or refer to someone who is an authority on a subject.

A Hawaiian kahuna, *circa 1890. (Source: Hawai'i State Archives)*

Kane

According to the accounts of missionaries and Europeans who first made documented contact with ancient Native Hawaiians, the god Kane was chief amongst their pantheon of gods. Kane was the great god of procreation and was also worshiped as the ancestor of both royalty (chiefs of different levels) and commoners. Kane plays a central figure in both the creation account of the world and in many versions of the Kumu-Honua, the legend of the first man on Earth.

Kane is said to have made three worlds, with the first being the upper heaven, a realm where gods dwell high above the earth. The second world would be the lower heaven, resting just above the earth, a place of the sky, stars, clouds, and rain. The third world would then be the garden of Earth, with mankind and all the animals and plants that were in it. After that, Kane is said to have made man out of a combination of clays. The right side of the man's head was made from clays of the north and east, while the left side of the head was made from clays of the south and west. Then, working together with the gods Ku and Lono, Kane and Ku breathed into the nostrils of the fashioned man, while Lono breathed into its mouth, thus giving man life. Many accounts of ancient Hawaiian myths and legends have too many similarities with biblical stories to be a coincidence. Indeed, many scholars see these accounts as having been painted with coloring and emphasis that is decidedly Christian, especially since some of the first Europeans who wrote about Native Hawaiian mythology were missionaries. However, after removing elements of Christianity that were probably inadvertently included, these accounts are not too far removed from the truth, as evidenced by their similarities to Tahitian creation myths.

Kane would be worshipped at *heiaus* without images for a long time. Some of the *heiaus* would have stones fashioned into a conical shape representing Kane, possibly with some paintings or carvings to further give the stone character. People would come and offer food and pray for forgiveness for any trespasses they might have made against the laws of the land. The Kane stone is also somewhat related to the shape of the male sexual organ, which is in line with Kane's generative powers over life and humanity. When worshiping Kane, families would have their own *'aumakua* (family god), and it would be reflected in the names of their own Kane god. The variety of these family god names would be extensive, numbering up to the thousands, but they all referred to the one god. Accordingly, in *heiaus*, there was one central altar at which to offer food and prayers.

One example of the myriad forms of Kane worship is the worship of Kane-hekili, meaning "Kane in the thunder." Native Hawaiians would worship Kane-hekili as an *'aumakua* on the island of Maui, along with other gods of thunder and lightning. When a heavy, loud storm would happen, legends say that it was customary to flip all containers upside down and to lie facedown, not making any sound. Silence during such heavy storms was considered the *tapu*

(law) of Kane-hekili. Yet another legend tells of O'ahu's Kaneana Cave, which has two stones resembling humanoid shapes. They are said to be the petrified forms of two boys that disobeyed their mother's instructions of keeping still and silent during the thunderstorm. Such customs would be observed by any family who claimed a thunder 'aumakua, thereby worshiping Kanehekili.

Many chiefs of early Hawai'i believe they were descended directly from Kane himself and are of the Ulu or Nanaulu line. These chiefs ranked higher than other chiefs, who had a less distinguished family genealogy. Such prestige came with the power to dictate *tapus* and judge offenses. Sometimes their authority would even approach divine status, and they would hold sway over matters of life and death. They would otherwise be known as *na li'i kapu akua*, or "chiefs with the tapus of gods."

Ku

Ku and Hina are the male and female forms, respectively, of the great ancestral gods of heaven and Earth. Linguistically, *Ku* means erect and to stand upright, whereas *Hina* means to lean and lay downward. Solar movements can also be labeled with these terms, with the rising sun being referred to as Ku and the setting sun being referred to as Hina.

Therefore, Ku is the expression of male generative power and virility. Hina is seen as the expression of female fertility and the power of growth and production. Together, they make up one inclusive whole, with Ku presiding over all the male spirits and gods and Hina over the female ones. Much like other phallic symbolism, Ku is represented as a pointed and upright stone, a *pohaku*, which has come to mean "stone or rock" in the Hawaiian language today. Hina's primordial female energy is symbolized with a flat, rounded stone that is lying down, which is called *papa*.

Carving of the god Ku in his form of the war-god Ku-kaʻili-moku, meaning "Ku, the Snatcher of Land." (Source: Flickr, jmcd303)

The family of gods that are given Ku names are many and cover things like forests, rain, fishing, and war, to name a few. Some examples of these are the god of war, Ku-nui-akea (Ku the supreme one); the god of fishing, Kuʻula (Ku of the bounties of the sea); and the god of the green land, Ku-olono-wao (Ku of the deep forest). The Ku gods of the forest would be worshiped by hunters and gatherers who ventured deep inland to gather wild food in times of scarcity and need. Canoe builders would pray to their canoe-building gods to help them with specific activities or hardships, like hollowing out a canoe with a bevel adze, a carpentry tool.

Kanaloa

While Kanaloa is often mentioned amongst the foremost of the gods of ancient Hawai'i, not much is known about him. Kanaloa is the god of the squid and might be connected to the god that breaks the evil influence of sorcery and black magic. However, Kanaloa is treated with a level of distrust that is uncommon for the chief gods of the Hawaiian pantheon. He is not invoked with the same level of trust and devotion as other *'aumakua*, and he is associated with certain qualities of deep and dark water. These qualities smack of uncertainty, danger, dark spirits, death, and other themes of the underworld. Various legends of strife and conflict with the god Kane are told in which Kanaloa and his subordinate spirits rebel against the gods of the sky, Kane in particular.

Although legend places Kane and Kanaloa in opposition as the good and evil gods of mankind, some legends show them as complementary halves of a whole. This is also evidenced by wider genealogies of similar gods across Polynesia, where they also hold dominion over the afterlife. These connections of death and creation show that Kane and Kanaloa were two necessary halves of the world, a philosophy that is not overly concerned with the dichotomy of good versus evil. In cultural activities and old chants, there exists a vast amount of mythical and religious lore that invokes Kane and Kanaloa together. Both gods were invoked by those involved with canoes, whether they were builders, explorers, or sailors, with Kane being for the consecration of newly built canoes and Kanaloa for sailing.

The island of Kaho'olawe is also said to belong to Kanaloa. Some chants and oral histories see the Tahitian god Ta'aroa, the contemporary or origin god of Kanaloa, as landing on the shores of Kaho'olawe and naming the island after himself. Additionally, Kane and Kanaloa are described as avid *awa* (kava) drinkers and water-finders, explorers, and cultivators of new islands.

Mythologically, both Kane and Kanaloa are described as gods who lived in the bodies of men.

Lono

Some scholars believe that Lono was a later fusion of the Tahitian gods Ro'o and Tane, with Ro'o being the messenger of Tane. They were the gods of the sky, clouds, rain, and storms. In Hawai'i, Lono is the influencer and master of clouds, thunder, lightning, and whirlwinds. Since the ancient Hawaiians were exposed to many interactions between winds, water, rain, and waves, they drew mythical and meteorological connections between phenomena like waterspouts, mountain springs, and cloud formations. These things were considered to be under the purview of the god Lono. As such, the order of priests worshiping Lono would set up *heiaus* to pray for rain and favorable weather conditions for sailing and fishing. The Lono priests existed well into the days of King Kamehameha, and they built *heiaus* and shrines to pray for deliverance from sicknesses and for abundant rain and crop growth.

A figure depicting the Hawaiian god Lono, circa 1790. (Source: Wikimedia Commons, Sailko. Original work exhibited at Arts of Oceania in the Louvre)

Pele

In 1840, the renowned American geologist James Dana correctly deduced that the islands of Hawai'i were formed from volcanic hotspot activity, with the youngest island being the "Big Island," the island of Hawai'i itself, and the oldest island being the island of Kaua'i. He deduced this from observations of the degrees of erosion of volcanic peaks on the islands.

This pattern of decreasing age going from northwest to the southeast of the Hawaiian island chain had already been recognized by ancient Hawaiians and is represented as such in the telling of the Pele legend.

It is said that the volcano goddess Pele and her family came from the land of Kahiki (Tahiti), which was regarded as a faraway mythical land to ancient Hawaiians. In the vein of Hawaiian mythology being centered around families and gods having a certain element that they are intimately connected with, Pele and her family looked to build a home of lava and fire in a volcanic hollow. She began digging on the island her family first landed on, the island of Ni'ihau. But for every deep and large hole she dug, groundwater would rush in and flood the pit, rendering it unsuitable for her and her family.

Pele continued with her efforts on all of the islands, making her way southward, only to have her efforts fail again and again. When she reached the island of Hawai'i, she was able to find a home for her family in the water-free pits of Moku'aweoweo and Halema'uma'u. Pele and her family made their abodes there in fiery homes of lava and magma. Today, those two pits lie in the calderas of Mauna Loa and Kilauea, respectively, with Mauna Loa being the largest active volcano on Earth and Kilauea being Hawai'i's most active volcano.

Halemaʻumaʻu crater, Kilauea volcano. (Source: Wikimedia Commons, Ivan Vtorov)

The volcanic origins of Hawaiʻi have largely been a boon for both ancient and Native Hawaiians. The rich mineral content makes for extremely fertile soil, and volcanic glass was an invaluable resource for ancient Hawaiians, who used the razor-sharp flakes for drills, cutting tools, and various other implements. Archaeological investigations also show that ancient Hawaiians had an extensive mining and quarry site near the southern summit of Mauna Kea, an area rich in fine-grained basalt. These were used to manufacture adze and other similar tools, even though the site was located in a dangerous and inhospitable environment.

Antennae covered with strands that seem like hair at Puʻu Oʻo, near Kilauea, Hawaiʻi. These hairs are thin, hardened strands of volcanic glass. In Hawaiʻi, they are called "lauoho o Pele" or "Pele's hair," and they are named after the goddess. (Source: United States Geological Survey)

Stones and boulders that resembled male and female genitalia often held special significance for ancient Hawaiians, and a few groupings of large boulders would be recognized as special "birthing stones." They would be visited by pregnant wives of chiefs and other pregnant female royalty. Oral traditions tell of how they would lay on top of these stones or touch and worship them to bring good fortune and health to both themselves and their babies. Such associations of formations of rocks and stones with deities and lesser gods were common in early Hawaiʻi. Some even formed the site of religious shrines, and other large stones were known as "bell stones," which would ring out sonorous tones when struck.

Chapter 4 – Point of Contact

Hawai'i's historical trajectory changed dramatically upon its contact with European explorers, which began with the arrival of British explorer Captain James Cook in 1778. Despite this being the most well-known and well-documented instance of Hawaiian contact with European travelers, Spanish archives have documentation of a fleet of conquistador ships sailing from the southern end of Mexico toward the Philippines that arrived at islands that resemble Hawai'i. Nonetheless, these findings and discoveries were not publicized or made widely known by Spain. In all likelihood, Spain kept the discovery of the Hawaiian Islands a secret to maintain supremacy over trading lines and to retain a naval advantage.

James Cook Arrives

Contested claims aside, James Cook is generally credited as being the first European to "discover" Hawai'i, and he made two trips to the island. He had already made two voyages around the globe, and on December 8th, 1777, he captained two armed ships, the *Discovery* and *Resolution*, to set out for the northwest coast of North America from the Society Islands, where Tahiti is. A month later, in January of 1778, James Cook landed on O'ahu and spotted the island of Kaua'i just ahead. The following days saw him sail toward Ni'ihau, and he eventually came into contact with local

Hawaiians on the southeastern side of Kauaʻi. The locals and James Cook bartered and exchanged vegetables and fish for nails and metal. Captain Cook was surprised by their friendliness and ability to speak a language not so different from the one spoken on the Society Islands.

Slowly, as the ships proceeded toward more agreeable coasts, the news spread amongst the natives, and excitement grew. James Cook made a note of large crowds of people gathering to see the novel sight of his ships, himself, and the other strange visitors. Upon trying to go ashore with three armed boats, some locals pressed onto James Cook's group too thickly and tried to take away their oars, muskets, and anything else that seemed interesting and modern. Cook's entourage was forced to fire a warning shot, killing one man but restoring a boundary of personal space between them and the natives in the process.

Eventually, the natives came to revere and even worshiped Captain Cook and his men, as they were seen as kings or beings with divine authority. When Captain Cook and his boats anchored at Waimea Bay, the natives brought forth offerings of captured pigs and plantain trees, and prayers were performed by priests and shamans. In return, Captain Cook gave them nails, knives, pieces of iron, and cloth, which pleased the natives greatly, as iron was a scarce resource and was seen as a precious metal. In fact, even sacred red feathers and cloaks that were reserved for royalty were offered to Captain Cook.

Eventually, he ventured inland with a few men, including his surgeon and the expedition's artist. He was followed by a train of natives, and he eventually walked up a valley to visit a *heiau*, of which he wrote descriptions and asked for a drawing to be made. Over the following days, Cook would visit the islands of Niʻihau and Kauaʻi. As he was leaving Kauaʻi, he was visited by a young chief w a high rank and his wife, and they exchanged presents with Captain Cook. Summarily, Cook's visit to the islands was met with the utmost respect, most likely out of a perception of divinity, and the people allowed him to collect fresh water, restock on provisions, and trade. This introduced melon, pumpkin, and onion seeds to the shores of Hawai'i, and his entire crew were, on the whole, treated very hospitably by the natives.

A drawing of a heiau *at Waimea, Kaua'i, that was done by John Webber, a member of* James Cook's expedition, circa 1778-1779. Engraved by D. K. Bonatti, after drawings by G. Gattina. (Source: Edward Joesting (1998), Kaua'i: The Separate Kingdom)

Return Trip

By all accounts, Native Hawaiians were quite perplexed by the character and appearance of their new visitors and held them in high regard and wonder. The majority of natives saw Captain Cook as an incarnation of the god Lono, who, as the natives and priests had previously foretold and supposed, had returned in a different form to fulfill ancient prophecies. They rightly suspected that Cook and his crew had come from Kahiki and the other mysterious lands to the south of Hawai'i. Oral descriptions of Cook and his men were sent to O'ahu, Maui, and the other islands by messengers. The messengers said that "these men are white, their skin is loose and wrinkled, their heads are angular and from their mouths they breathe smoke and fire. Their bodies have openings into which they thrust their hands and bring out beads, nails, pieces of iron and other treasures. Their speech is unintelligible."

Captain Cook's second visit to Hawai'i came in the year 1779 after exploring the coast of Alaska and the Bering Strait and charting regions of the Arctic Ocean. Indeed, James Cook was a spectacular navigator and cartographer. Cook spent a few weeks sailing around the islands of Hawai'i, eventually anchoring in Kealakekua Bay. Records tell of an elderly priest venerating Cook's return with royal symbols of red feathered cloaks and valuable offerings. Upon landing, Cook was conducted to a *heiau* dedicated to the god Lono, where he was subjected to various ceremonies, and an image of him was installed as an incarnation of the god. Afterward, he was followed by priests and met with veneration and worship wherever he went, as priests would follow him with wands and advise the locals to prostrate themselves.

Around this time, the king of Hawai'i, Kalani'opu'u, was engaged in a war with a challenger for the throne, Kahekili. A few days after Cook's landing, King Kalani'opu'u made a grand visit to the ships of Captain Cook, bringing along three large canoes and bearing gifts of wickerwork idols that were adorned with jewelry. The idols were inlaid with mother of pearl and shark teeth. Captain Cook received the royal party on board the *Resolution* and presented the king with linen shirts and a handsome cutlass. Captain Cook also presented a firework show, which impressed the natives greatly, for they had never seen such things before.

Even so, the locals eventually began to tire of hosting Captain Cook and his men, as the newcomers were not aware of the local taboos and customs, which were called *kapu*. In fact, the

Polynesian concept of *tapu* is where we derive our word "taboo" from. These violations by James Cook and his men would sow seeds of doubt about their supposedly divine nature, and the men were met with disgust. The lavish gifts also began to become burdensome and expensive, as meat and fresh produce were luxuries that were labor-intensive to procure. The death of one of the European sailors had also further disillusioned the natives' view of the men as incarnations of gods. As a result, quarrels and disputes over trading and exchanges became more and more common, gradually escalating into thefts and small fights.

Early in February of 1779, King Kalani'opu'u presented Captain Cook with an immense number of vegetables, an entire herd of swine, and an extensive collection of clothing and barkcloth. Cook was astonished at the volume and magnitude of the present, which was probably intended as a farewell gift meant to send them off. Captain Cook departed shortly after the gift was presented to him, and he set his sights on the Leeward Islands in the Caribbean. Unfortunately, he was met with a violent gale, and the *Resolution* damaged her foremast, forcing them to return to Kealakekua Bay for repairs. What greeted them was "an ominous silence everywhere...with not a canoe in sight." A boat sent ashore brought back news to Captain Cook that King Kalani'opu'u was absent and had placed the bay under *kapu*, effectively making the bay forbidden. Canoes with provisions were supplied, but the friendly manner that was previously expressed was nowhere to be found, and iron daggers were demanded in return for the provisions.

Shortly after, matters worsened, as a few natives stole some metal implements from the *Discovery*, either in retaliation for a perceived slight or for want of iron and metal. Palea, a chief who had been tasked with overseeing the people, went after the thieves, and a fight broke out between the natives and sailors that soured relations even more. That following night, a large and fast boat of the *Discovery* was stolen by the natives and broken up for the iron that held it together.

This caused Captain Cook to try and kidnap King Kalaniʻopuʻu and hold him prisoner until the stolen boat was returned. Such a tactic had worked for Cook before on other islands in the south. Thus, he went ashore with a lieutenant and nine sailors and headed toward Kalaniʻopuʻu's house. Cook's plan was to invite him to come aboard the *Resolution* and spend the day with him. Captain Cook's men had also formed a blockade of the bay with three boats that were well-armed and manned. Unfortunately, while Captain Cook was trying to invite King Kalaniʻopuʻu onto the *Resolution*, a canoe that knew nothing of the blockade came into the bay and was fired upon. Kalimu, the brother to Chief Palea, was killed, and news of his death was quickly sent to the king and his guards.

As a large crowd of armed natives gathered to bar Captain Cook's way back onto his ship, the king slowly realized that Captain Cook was his enemy. Captain Cook and his men tried to launch their boats and flee, but a fight ensued. Rocks, daggers, and swords were thrown, which resulted in Captain Cook being stabbed to death and four other sailors dying. Lieutenant John Gore, who was on board the *Resolution*, saw what was happening with his spyglass and ordered several cannon rounds to be shot into the crowd that was chasing the fleeing men. The aftermath saw seventeen natives killed. Captain Cook's body was taken to a *heiau*, and funerary rites were performed. His flesh was removed to be burned, and his bones were cleaned and deified. Eventually, some of his remains were taken by friendly priests to be given back to the sailors.

The Captain Cook memorial site, which says "Near This Spot Capt. James Cook Met His *Death February 14 1779." (Source: Wikimedia Commons, gillfoto)*

Even after his death, the journals and writings of James Cook brought many other explorers and sailors to the islands of Hawai'i, forever changing the lives of Native Hawaiians. Cook's unexpected death dissuaded other expeditions toward the Hawaiian Islands for over seven years, and in this time, Hawai'i was separated into three smaller kingdoms following the breakup of Kalani'opu'u's kingdom. Around the year 1780, Kalani'opu'u held a great council among his high chiefs to settle the succession of his kingdom, and among those present was Kalani'opu'u's nephew, Kamehameha. Kamehameha was appointed the religious leader and representative of the Hawaiian god of war, Ku-ka'ili-moku. King Kalani'opu'u died in the spring of 1782, and the redistribution of lands was customary after the passing of a *mo'i*, or great ruler. Chaos and power struggles followed his passing, and many fights and rebellions followed in the years to come.

More to Come

Part of the narrative of Captain Cook's last voyages showed the potential profits that could be made by trading and exploration. Fur traders reaped in profits from trading with the Native Americans of the northwest coast of America. Expeditions from India, England, China, and various parts of the Americas set out to engage in this trade, with the main rendezvous point being Vancouver Island. The island was located just above what is now the northern border between the United States of America and Canada. The small body of water that lay on the western edge of Vancouver Island was called Nootka Sound, with "sound" meaning a part of the sea that turns into an inlet of sorts.

The first recorded ships that visited the Hawaiian Islands after the death of James Cook were the *King George*, which was commanded by Captain Nathaniel Portlock, and the *Queen Charlotte*, which was commanded by Captain George Dixon. Both of these commanders had served under Captain Cook before and set off from London to sail together. They were not welcome at Kealakekua Bay and went toward Oʻahu instead, anchoring themselves in Waiʻalae Bay. Around the same time, a French explorer reached the eastern shores of Maui near Honuaʻula. Dixon and Portlock bought food and fresh water with iron nails and metal weapons. Captain Portlock also noted that almost all of the iron daggers that were sold, traded, and gifted by Captain Cook had ended up in the hands of Kahekili and his warriors. A few months later, Dixon and Portlock visited the islands of Hawaiʻi again in 1786, trading hoops of iron, beads, and nails for provisions, wood, and water. They made land at Waiʻalae, Oʻahu, and Waimea, Kauaʻi, before moving on toward China.

One of the notable visits to Kauaʻi was the *Nootka*, a ship that was led by Captain John Meares. After spending a month at Kauaʻi, a famous chief named Kaʻiana went with Captain Meares as a passenger, where they continued toward Canton, China, now known as modern-day Guangzhou. Kaʻiana was known to Captain Portlock as Tyanna, an Anglicized form of the Hawaiian pronunciation, and he was a tall man. Kaʻiana was a guest of his English friends and had a warm and hospitable stay. Because of his tall stature and his feathered cape and helmet, Kaʻiana would walk the streets of Canton and terrify the local Chinese people with his imposing figure.

After three months, Captain Meares outfitted and commissioned two vessels, the *Felice Adventurer* and *Iphigenia*, to further carry out fur trades and take Kaʻiana and three other natives as passengers. Kaʻiana boarded *Iphigenia*, which was commanded by Captain William Douglas, and Kaʻiana arrived back on the island of Hawaiʻi at Kealakekua Bay, where he was greeted by Kamehameha. The welcoming party consisted of twelve large double canoes that were beautifully decorated and adorned. Unfortunately, Kamehameha brought news that Kaʻeo, the king of Kauaʻi, had turned hostile toward Kaʻiana, and Kaʻiana accepted

Kamehameha's offer to enter into his service as a form of protection. At this time, the Hawaiian Islands were plagued by warfare and instability, and Kamehameha recognized the advantage of having a chief who was learned and familiar with foreign ways on his side. Kaʻiana was granted a large property to live on and oversee as his own territory on the island of Hawaiʻi. In return, Kaʻiana's collection of foreign goods, tools, and firearms was now under the indirect control of Kamehameha.

Kamehameha Rising

Shortly after landing on the island of Hawaiʻi, Kaʻiana asked Captain Douglas to gift Kamehameha a swivel cannon to be mounted on a large double canoe. After much persuasion, Captain Douglas relented. This was one of the first recorded instances of Kamehameha compiling firearms and gathering his military strength.

King Kamehameha I depicted at spear practice. (Source: Brother Bertram Photo Collection, Gabriel Bertram Bellinghausen)

In particular, a high chief and counselor to Kamehameha named Kameʻeiamoku ambushed an American ship, the *Fair American*, in retaliation for earlier offenses by another American vessel, the *Eleanor*, which was captained by Simon Metcalfe. Captain Metcalfe had also used the *Eleanor* to massacre over one hundred innocent natives at Olowalu, Maui, in 1790 because Olowalu was the home village of the suspected thieves of one of Captain Metcalfe's boats. This incident would go on to be known as the Olowalu Massacre. By coincidence, the *Fair American* was captained by Simon Metcalfe's son, Thomas Metcalfe.

The *Fair American* was seized, and Thomas Metcalfe was killed, along with almost all of the crew. The only survivor was Isaac Davis, who was a mate aboard the ship, and he was rounded up with John Young, a detained boatswain who was previously aboard the *Eleanora*. These two would be treated with kindness and generosity by Kameʻeiamoku because Kamehameha wanted them on his side for their expertise in handling muskets and cannons. They were raised to the rank of chief and paid for their services in war and their counsel. Troops of men were trained by Young and Davis in musketry and shooting, and in time, they would prove to be invaluable advisors and generals for King Kamehameha.

Thereafter, Kamehameha sent a summons to Keoua Kuʻahuʻula, a son of the former King Kalaniʻopuʻu, and Keawemaʻuhili, who was the half-brother to King Kalaniʻopuʻu, making him Kamehameha's uncle, for more men and canoes. Keoua Kuʻahuʻula refused, but Kamehameha was backed by his uncle Keawemaʻuhili, who sent men along with his own sons.

With this, Kamehameha finally felt strong enough to invade and take over the island of Maui.

After consolidating a large force of men and canoes, Kamehameha crossed the channel in the summer of 1790 and landed in Hana and then Hamakualoa. Here, he defeated the vanguard of the Maui forces and moved his fleet to Kahului, where he eventually clashed with the Maui army, which was led by Kahekili's sons. The two field artillery squads that were led by Young and Davis, along with Kamehameha's significant advantage in musketry and firepower, pushed the Maui warriors back and broke their morale. Kamehameha was victorious and showed no mercy to the vanquished factions, driving them over cliffs and forcing them to barricade themselves in crags and caves, where they were starved out.

However, Kamehameha's conquest of Maui was not permanent. Due to his absence on the island of Hawaiʻi, Keoua Kuʻahuʻula invaded the district of Hilo and killed Keawemaʻuhili. Upon hearing this news, Kamehameha sailed back with all of his forces from Molokaʻi to Hawaiʻi, landing at Kawaihae. The resulting battles pushed Keoua Kuʻahuʻula back and forced a retreat, but the battles were indecisive.

Kamehameha fell back to Waipiʻo to recover from his losses, while Keoua Kuʻahuʻula fell back to Hilo, where he began planning his next move. Finally, in November 1790, Keoua Kuʻahuʻula set out on an overland route that passed by the volcano Kilauea. He and his forces made camp there for two days, even though the crater was showing signs of activity. As luck would have it, Kilauea erupted on the third day, spewing noxious clouds of black sand, hot cinder, and bits of lava. The terrific earthquake and destructive shower killed more than half of Keoua Kuʻahuʻula's men and forced him to move before he was ready. Kamehameha saw the eruption as a divine sign from the goddess Pele that he was the rightful heir of Hawaiʻi.

A year later, in 1791, Kamehameha finally captured and killed Keoua Kuʻahuʻula, who had all but given up the struggle. Kamehameha had Keoua and some of his warriors sacrificed to the god of war, Ku-kaʻili-moku, at the Puʻukohola Heiau. This made Kamehameha the undisputed master of the island of Hawaiʻi.

Ruins of the Puʻukohola Heiau. Image taken in 2007. (Source: Wikimedia Commons, Bamse)

Kahekili would pass away in July of 1794, making his descendants, relatives, and other chiefs fight and quarrel over matters in his absence. Subsequently, his kingdom would fall into chaos, and since it was so spread out and disunited, the lands all fell one by one to Kamehameha. In

1795, due to infighting between Kahekili's eldest son, Kalanikupule, and other family members, Kamehameha saw that the time had now come to conquer the other islands. Mustering up all his arms and men, Kamehameha commanded what was probably the largest and best-equipped army that the Hawaiian archipelago had seen at that time. Kamehameha's war party would sail to Lahaina, Maui, and raze the west coast. The commanding chief, Koalaukane, had fled to O'ahu without putting up any resistance. Kamehameha would then move on Moloka'i. His battle with the troops on O'ahu would be fierce, but Kamehameha would prevail, making him master of all the islands except Kaua'i and Ni'ihau.

Before launching his attack on Kaua'i and Ni'ihau, Kamehameha employed foreign mechanics to build him a massive vessel that weighed forty tons and was armed with many four-pound cannons. In spite of his plans, Kamehameha did not wait to complete this ship before sailing for war on Kaua'i. He had dedicated and consecrated a *heiau* in Ewa with human sacrifices and moved his army and fleet to Wai'anae. From there, they sailed under cover of night to Kaua'i, but the fleet encountered a fierce tempest that wrecked many of his canoes and forced them back to Wai'anae.

During this time, Kamehameha was also facing a rebellion against his authority back on the island of Hawai'i. This caused him to sail back to Hawai'i with the bulk of his forces and crush the rising rebellion. This was the last of Kamehameha's wars, and it put to rest any other thoughts of challenging his rule. Since the island of Ni'ihau did not possess many resources or opposition,

Kamehameha ignored it and eventually negotiated a peaceful unification between the lands he ruled with the island of Kaua'i. He cemented his position as the first king of a united Hawai'i, which would be called the Kingdom of Hawai'i.

Statue of King Kamehameha I in the hall of the United States Capitol. (Source: Wikimedia Commons, Alacoolwiki)

Chapter 5 – The Kingdom of Hawai'i

Although the concept of land ownership is markedly different for Native Hawaiians than Europeans, for example, it is still accurate to say that the history of Hawaiian lands is a history of those lands moving from the hands of Native Hawaiian people into the hands of others.

Different Systems of Tenure

A successive chain of Native Hawaiian monarchs tried valiantly to retain their sovereignty over the lands of Hawai'i, but they were ultimately unsuccessful. This pattern of political development is not atypical; almost every other group of islands in the Pacific also fell to Western rule over the course of a few hundred years. For example, de facto control over New Zealand was slowly given over to Great Britain, first through a treaty signed by Māori chiefs in 1840 and then by the chiefs of Fiji, who transferred sovereignty over to Queen Victoria in 1874. Great Britain would go on to claim Tuvalu and Kiribati, followed by the southern Solomon Islands, as their territories or protectorates.

Before European influence and political maneuvers, the prevailing system of land ownership was a native-centric arrangement that was complex and based on interdependent agricultural and societal needs. This was expressed in a spirit of reciprocity between the people and the land, or *'aina*. *'Aina* was not something that could be traded, sold, or bought. It is more accurate to say that the land was to be controlled through a system of joint responsibility and accountability that was to be managed by the chiefs of Hawai'i, the *ali'i*. The Hawaiian system of land tenure perceived any handling of land in a transactional manner to be debasing to both one's family and themselves. As such, even the chiefs and kings were only to deal with land distribution and portioning merely as trustees of a higher authority.

Death by Disease

Tragically, the foreigners to Hawai'i brought many germs, pathogens, and viruses that infected the local native population. The islands of Hawai'i had long been isolated from the rest of the world with little to no contact with emerging pathogens. This meant that the people of Hawai'i were very susceptible and vulnerable to these foreign diseases. Further worsening the problem was the tight social connections and communal lifestyles that were the cultural norm of the Hawaiians, leading to fast-spreading outbreaks.

Additionally, there was a marked scarcity in the supply of doctors, and epidemics ravaged the Native Hawaiians in waves. By the 1800s, the native population had been utterly devastated. Venereal diseases such as gonorrhea and syphilis ran rampant due to no effective treatment being available at the time. It is suspected that these viruses and infections, which were colloquially given the nickname of the "Curse of Cook," were a major factor in the drastic drop of the Native Hawaiians' birthrate. Moreover, sicknesses like tuberculosis, leprosy, and scabies made life very uncomfortable, painful, and scary. Dysentery, cholera, and typhoid fever further served to weaken the population, so much so that sudden deaths were commonplace. Family members might go a few days without seeing another relative, only to realize they had passed away while working, gathering food, or going about their daily activities. Local estimates put the number of deaths over the years as "cutting the population in half," which modern analysis confirms.

Hawaiians lacked the immunities that were adapted via exposure that many of their Western visitors and guests had, meaning they succumbed to the common cold and flu at a much higher rate. Measles and mumps outbreaks also occurred and resulted in childhood deaths and further population decline. In the 1850s, despite the best preventive efforts of visiting captains, traders, and merchants, a smallpox outbreak infected well over six thousand Hawaiians and resulted in thousands of deaths.

Such a drastic and irreparable decline in native peoples, combined with the slow and steady influx of foreigners and their culture, caused an increasing state of disorder and confusion in the Kingdom of Hawai'i. As individuals died and their plots of land were abandoned, people from rural communities slowly began to leave and move closer to the expanding urban centers. Trading, medicine, and social support were more readily available in the more densely populated places. The more isolated villages and farms were neglected and abandoned, as the amount of manpower a community or family had slowly decreased and, with it, their capacity for farming and supporting themselves.

Changing Religions

The palpable desperation that permeated Hawai'i because of the consecutive waves of epidemics caused a significant change in the religious composition of the islands. People who sought treatment and answers from their traditional priests and shamans were not satisfied with what they received. Hawaiians relied on their spiritual heritage and depended on their healers and leaders to show them a way to survive these troubled times. Additionally, old-standing religious beliefs would be challenged by the arrival and proselytization of Christian missionaries. Many Native Hawaiians converted to Christianity, mostly either as entire families or as individuals who did not have anywhere else to go.

An artist's depiction of the Ahu'ena Heiau in 1816. (Source: Louis Choris)

Another big factor in the gradual discontinuation of the old ways was the effect of two leading female *ali'i*, who challenged the status quo and the status of *kapu*. These two individuals were Ka'ahumanu and Keopuolani, both of whom were wives of King Kamehameha I. Polygamy was more common for Hawaiian royalty than it was for normal Hawaiians, with high-ranking chiefs and kings having multiple wives. Ka'ahumanu and Keopuolani were politically powerful and saw the *kapu* system as oppressive to women, and they detested it. They pushed harder to abolish the system after King Kamehameha I's death, and Kamehameha II, who was the son of King Kamehameha I, decided to support his mother and end numerous *kapu* practices. These included the end of various task segregations by sex and also implicitly allowed more of the missionary-led destruction of many temples and idols of the islands to occur. This extraordinary event was a landmark moment, for "the Hawai'i of old" was no more. Historians and scholars today also strongly believe that the move to abolish these old systems also allowed the Kamehameha dynasty to further protect their political supremacy by ensuring other chiefs no longer had access to the traditional ways of gaining or claiming rank, prestige, or sociocultural approval.

Queen Ka'ahumanu with her servant, a painting by Louis Choris, 1816. (Source: Plate III in Louis Choris's Voyage Pittoresque Autour du Monde, Paris, 1822. Hawai'i State Archives)

This "spiritual power vacuum" was promptly filled by Protestant missionaries, especially once a group of Calvinists that hailed from the American Board of Commissioners for Foreign Missions got permission from King Kamehameha II to stay on the islands. These missionaries soon set out for O'ahu and Kaua'i, and they slowly gained followers and political power. They accomplished this very effectively by establishing schools and teaching the English language and system of writing. These new opportunities for employment, housing, learning, and a place of belonging attracted many Native Hawaiians to the newcomers. The missionaries also claimed that the reason the diseases ravaged the islanders so brutally was their failure to believe in Jesus Christ and his divine message. Eventually, Queen Keopuolani became the first *aliʻi* to officially convert to Christianity in 1823.

The Tragic Trip

In an effort to thank King George IV for the gift of a gunship, King Kamehameha II traveled to London aboard the British whaling ship *L'Aigle* in 1823. He also intended for the trip to foster closer diplomatic ties between his budding kingdom and the British. On the way, the ship arrived at Rio de Janeiro to visit the newly independent Empire of Brazil and exchange luxurious gifts with Emperor Pedro I. Unbeknownst to both parties, both the Empire of Brazil and the Kingdom of Hawaiʻi would eventually fall. Nonetheless, King Kamehameha II and his wife, Queen Kamamalu, arrived in Portsmouth six months after they had set sail from Hawaiʻi. They were moved into the Caledonian Hotel in London and greeted hospitably by members of the British government. However, the local press treated their arrival with confusion and ridicule, misspelling King Kamehameha II's birthname (Liholiho) name and making fun of the Hawaiian Islands.

Rhio Rhio, King of the Sandwich Islands, *a sketch done in London by an unknown artist with a misspelling of Liholiho's name. (Source: Samuel Kamakau,* Ruling Chiefs of Hawaii, *1992)*

    Regardless, King Kamehameha II and his entourage toured London and were well looked after by their hosts. They visited Westminster Abbey, attended ballet and opera shows at the Royal Opera House and the Theatre Royal, and also had portraits made of them. King Kamehameha II was said to be quite a sight for the British people, as he was over six feet tall, well-built, and dark-skinned. Unfortunately, both King Kamehameha II and his queen contracted measles and had no immunity to the disease. Queen Kamamalu died on July 8th, 1824, and her grief-stricken husband passed away six days later on July 14th. Their bodies were kept in the crypt of an Anglican church and later returned back to Hawaiʻi aboard the Royal Navy frigate the HMS *Blonde.* King

Kamehameha II's brother, Kauikeaouli, succeeded the throne of the Kingdom of Hawai'i and became King Kamehameha III.

The Continuation of the Kingdom

The untimely death of King Kamehameha II and his queen in London only served to solidify the powers and influence of missionaries in Hawaiian society. This was further demonstrated when the procession of King Kamehameha II's body was led with Anglican prayers, including similar prayers said in the Hawaiian language. Before his departure, King Kamehameha II had named his brother to be the ruler in his absence, but since Kauikeaouli was only nine years old, Ka'ahumanu, the wife of King Kamehameha I, assumed control of the Kingdom of Hawai'i. She shared power with another high chief named Kalanimoku, who was her cousin. Kalanimoku was also known as Karaimoku and reputedly had great political and business acumen. This earned him the nickname "the Iron Cable of Hawai'i."

Kauikeaouli, or King Kamehameha III, would come to power after the death of Ka'ahumanu, which happened when he was eighteen years old. He inherited all of the former problems of his predecessors. His subjects continued to suffer immensely from disease epidemics, and foreigners continued to badger and demand more goods and produce from the islands, along with allotments of land. Interestingly, King Kamehameha III decided to embrace older cultural traditions and worked to secure his kingdom against foreign interests for the good of his people. His upbringing saw him torn between the Christian teachings of Ka'ahumanu and the old Hawaiian traditions. He was influenced by a young Hawaiian-Tahitian priest named Kaomi, with whom King Kamehameha III was also intimate. Intimate same-sex relationships, *moe aikane*, were common among Hawaiian royalty and were accepted as normal and natural by Hawaiians for hundreds of years. This relationship earned Kamehameha III the anger and disapproval of the Christian missionaries.

A portrait of King Kamehameha III. (Source: Hawai'i State Archives)

King Kamehameha III worked to reinvigorate the cultural traditions of his people, and he encouraged them to partake in pre-colonial pastimes like hula, games, kava drinking, and other practices that were discouraged and forbidden by the Christian missionaries. This caused some amount of strife between *ali'i* that were Christian and other chiefs who were not. King Kamehameha III would try to ease tensions and bridge the divide by providing younger chiefs and *aliʻi* with formal Western schooling and language lessons. Through this, King Kamehameha III hoped to increase their flexibility and mediating ability when it came to complex issues that involved both Hawaiian and Westernized parts of society. He asked the American Missionary Society for a teacher to educate royal children, and they provided a teacher and his wife, which led to the establishment of a special school in Hawaiʻi for children of royal lineage.

King Kamehameha III also encoded many laws into actual text-based legislation. This was one of his most important contributions, as he helped codify the native rights of the Hawaiian people, especially the *makaʻainana*. Despite that, foreigners began increasingly demanding land, whether through their businesses or through economically-driven political interests. As the number of foreigners arriving on the Hawaiian Islands increased, so did the pressure on Hawaiian rulers and leaders to grant them some form of land ownership, whether to protect foreign capital investments or to provide new job opportunities for local Hawaiians.

This eventually drove King Kamehameha III to make the Declaration of Rights of 1839, which was followed very closely by the Constitution of 1840. Both of these are incredibly important documents in the history of Hawaiʻi. These documents were designed to protect the interests of all inhabitants of the kingdom and made drastic changes to the authority of the chiefs and head chiefs. These documents prohibited the oppression of the *makaʻainana* and stipulated that any chief or head chief who violated its laws must be removed from their position of power. The Declaration of Rights states that "it is not proper to enact laws that protect and enrich the rulers only, without regard to the enriching of their subjects also." Centrally, the Declaration put forth property rights for the people of Hawaiʻi, securing their lands for them. It states that as long as they conformed to the laws of the Kingdom of Hawaiʻi, nothing may be taken from them.

These documents were notable because they were not passed under duress or by an unwilling sovereign. Instead, it was a wise decision by a prudent ruler. King Kamehameha III understood the new wave of logic, needs, and principles that were being brought forth by Western norms, and the passing of these documents clearly heralded a new age in the civilization of his kingdom. Further, the 1840 Constitution explains the very concept of traditional Hawaiian thought as it pertains to land ownership, stating that although the land had belonged to King Kamehameha I, it was not his private property. He was merely the head of the management of that landed property. Such explicit acknowledgment of the relationship between the *ali'i*, the *maka'ainana*, and the lands of Hawai'i by this constitution was an important milestone in Native Hawaiian rights.

Sadly, representatives of foreign powers continued insisting on lands to lease and rent. These major foreign powers, namely the United States, Great Britain, and France, disguised their requests and demands as concerns over their citizens not being able to secure the future of their capital investments and to lease land for a fee. At times, these demands would be supported by the presence of warships. Spurred on by visits from the French and the Americans, an admiral of the Royal Navy, Lord George Paulet, sailed his warship to Honolulu in 1843 and made several demands under threat of violence and force. These demands included debt payments and legal rights for British subjects. The Hawaiian government was forced to accede to his demands, and King Kamehameha III signed an agreement stating as such. Paulet then destroyed every Hawaiian flag he could find and raised the British Union Flag during his period of occupation. Approximately five months later, the land would be surrendered back to the Kingdom of Hawai'i by British Rear Admiral Richard Thomas, who negotiated financial settlements and resolved the disputes of sovereignty over the land.

A picture of George Paulet, who was promoted to rear admiral on July 21ˢᵗ, 1856. (Source: Hawai'i State Archives)

This was clearly worrisome for the future of the Kingdom of Hawai'i, and it caused King Kamehameha III great distress. With the instability of political and military powers in the Hawaiian archipelago, he consulted his foreign advisors and missionaries on what he should do to protect the kingdom's sovereignty and ensure Hawaiian control of the land. Clearly, foreign powers wanted Hawai'i's system of land tenure to transition to one of private ownership for their own benefit, as they were familiar with such a system and wanted to obtain secure land titles. They further promoted such changes by pointing out that it would be a great help in steering the islands toward economic prosperity and encourage hard work. Predictably, large numbers of Hawaiian natives were deeply suspicious of the proposed changes and continually petitioned King Kamehameha III to reconsider his position on the matter. The local chiefs and residents were hesitant to compete with foreigners, as the change to the land tenure system would be confusing and difficult. Regardless, the Land Commission and King Kamehameha III proceeded with the Mahele process.

The Great Mahele

As the great foreign powers of Great Britain, the United States, and France vied over the muchcoveted lands and ports of Hawai'i and other territories in the Pacific region, Hawai'i experienced increasing political, military, and economic pressure from all sides. In line with many of his foreign advisors' counsel, King Kamehameha III realized that he had to assuage the demands for land from the Westerners, especially the ones who were already living in the Kingdom of Hawai'i.

King Kamehameha III was greatly beloved by his people and was considered to be one of Hawai'i's greatest rulers. This was partly because he stood astride both Western and Hawaiian cultures, being raised with Christian teachings and having learned the ways of Western politics. He was learned in English but simultaneously focused on promoting and giving his people back their old traditions and cultural identity. Historians note that he ensured no laws enforced any class distinctions and that he also carried forward the annulment of the *kapu* system that his mother had started during her period as queen regent.

In 1845, King Kamehameha III approved of the creation of a complex governmental group that is usually referred to as the Land Commission. This group consisted of a number of native and foreign lawyers, chiefs, businessmen, and legislators. They were in charge of overseeing land claims and disputes. Over time, it came to pass that there was to be a Great Division, also known as the Great Mahele, which was intended to be an overarching legal restructuring of the lands of Hawai'i and their tenure system. King Kamehameha III would retain his own lands, and he would divide the remainder of lands into thirds that would be given to the government, the *ali'i* (chiefs), and the *maka'ainana* (common people). King Kamehameha III's own land claims would be subject to dispute and residential claims, but most of the king's lands were not contested. Many *ali'i* relinquished certain parts of their lands or interests to King Kamehameha III, and the king did the same with respect to the plots of land that the *ali'i* wanted.

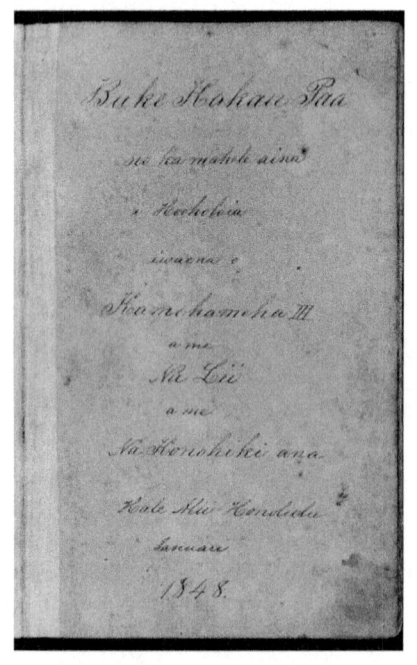

The title page of the Mahele Book, the record of the Great Mahele transaction, 1848. (Source: Hawai'i State Archives, Department of Accounting and General Services) In 1848, the divisional claims were completed, and King Kamehameha III held titles to almost

2.5 million acres of land, which amounted to around 60 percent of the Kingdom of Hawai'i.

However, King Kamehameha III ceded about 1.5 million acres to the government in order to satisfy demands and alleviate the economic and political burdens of his people. These 1.5 million acres came to be known as the "Government Lands" and were, in theory, also subject to the disputes and counterclaims of the *maka'ainana*. Summarily, the ruler held about 24 percent of the land, the government held about 37 percent of the land, and the remaining 39 percent was allotted to the *ali'i*. The underlying idea was for the *ali'i* to give up roughly half of the lands that they had titles for to the *maka'ainana* and the remainder to be made up through disputes, claims, and donations.

Unfortunately, the people of Hawai'i came to possess very little land in the end. They ended up being the clear losers over the course of the Great Mahele. Many of the *ali'i* ended up selling off their lands and land titles, whether by choice or by force. Subsequently, many of the *maka'ainana* who were reliant on the land rights of their *ali'i* were left homeless and lost their native tenancies. Many of the common people were confused and uninformed about what to do to obtain their land. They still largely believed in and operated by the traditional notion of land ownership, thinking they always had access to whatever lands they needed to survive and live. In fact, many preferred the old system and refused to change. Due to this friction, the government met to discuss the shortcomings of the Mahele process and adopted four resolutions that would be collectively known as the Kuleana Act of 1850. This act encouraged the *maka'ainana* to file claims with the Land Commission and extended the deadline. Still, these supplementary policies and reforms did not end up benefiting the people of Hawai'i much. Filing claims was a tedious and long process that was not explained to the Hawaiian masses. Furthermore, a claim could only be filed after a survey had been arranged and paid for, along with two witnesses to validate the entire thing. This cost money that a lot of people did not have, and reports from this time note an utter lack of qualified surveyors in the Kingdom of Hawai'i. As a result, the claims and surveys often became a matter of bribery and fraud, with many instances of favoritism, intentional delays, inconsistencies, and conflicts of interest. The Land Commission also did not establish clear rules or regulations to help smooth the process along, and many claims were rejected or left incomplete.

In total, over 14,000 claims were filed, but only about 8,400 were approved, which means roughly only 30 percent of the Native Hawaiians gained titles and rights. The average amount of land granted was about three acres, which meant that out of the millions of acres that were supposed to be distributed amongst the people of Hawai'i, less than twenty-nine thousand acres were actually given out. In other words, the Native Hawaiian commoners owned approximately 1 percent of Hawai'i's land area. The total amount that was owned was small enough to fit on the island of Kaho'olawe. By comparison, thirty-three missionary families had obtained roughly forty-one thousand acres of land.

Chapter 6 – The United States and Hawai'i

Any history of Hawai'i would be woefully incomplete without the inclusion of a specific chapter dedicated to the long history and relationship between the United States of America and Hawai'i. The effect of American culture on Hawai'i was so marked that from the 1800s onward, most cities and major towns of Hawai'i looked more American.

The streets were lined with churches, schools, commercial buildings, and residences that were fashioned after Western architecture and layouts. The language, music, and laws of Hawai'i were Americanized, sporting only hints and influences of native culture. Indisputably, Hawai'i was the subject of marketing, with ads touting a tropical and exotic paradise that also happened to have bottled beer, billiard tables, and tracks for horse cars.

Much of these influences can be attributed to the arrival of Christian missionaries, with most sources agreeing that this began with the arrival of seventeen Protestant missionaries in 1820. Like most Christian missionary writings of first contact with native peoples all over the world, the Hawaiian people were regarded and described by the Protestant missionaries as "dirty, lazy, spiritually ignorant and wild" people. Such a description was plainly false, as Native Hawaiians were decidedly industrious, especially from an exploratory and agricultural perspective. They had deep spiritual roots and had extensive cultural and social norms, which were all built around an extended unit of the family.

A mission school in Lahaina, Maui, 1909. (Source: The Spirit of Missions, *1909. Episcopal Church, Board of Missions)*

Nonetheless, there is strong evidence that points to the fact that Hawai'i is unmistakably American in feeling and action. Perhaps the largest objections to such claims are the historical track record of maltreatment of Native Hawaiians by foreigners and Americans, as well as the huge population of Japanese people living on the islands. The second point was a sore subject in the eyes of mainland Americans when schools kept the Japanese language. Japan also launched propaganda aimed at sowing discord amongst the Americans.

Western Influence

Hawai'i was no stranger to Western political agendas, which were inflicted onto many island nations in the Pacific. In reality, many powers tried to wrest control of the Hawaiian Islands from the natives. Very early on, in 1794, Captain George Vancouver (after whom the city of Vancouver is named) claimed the islands for Great Britain and hoisted its flag on several of the islands. However, his reports and actions were not ratified by London in time to be of any practical use. Furthermore, the Russians had also staked a claim over the islands of Hawai'i. The governor of Alaska at that time sent a vessel to Honolulu, ordering the construction of buildings that were fitted with mounted guns. They, too, hoisted the Russian flag over these buildings. Fortunately, King Kamehameha I built a large fort in Honolulu and expelled the Russians, eventually causing the Russian government to disavow their Russian agents. As the decades passed, the English residents of Hawai'i did not approve of or enjoy the American occupation of the islands. They frequently demanded meetings and consultations with American officials. The American presence was bolstered by the USS *Mohican*, a steampowered warship that was originally assigned to the Pacific Squadron but was later assigned to patrol and reinforce Hawai'i in the late 1880s.

The French also threatened war with King Kamehameha III in 1839 if the king did not relax the laws restricting the activities of French Catholic missionaries. Once the French had taken over the Marquesas Islands and established their own protectorate over Tahiti, they set their sights on the islands of Hawai'i and began disputing the claims of the British residents and officers of the Hawaiian Islands. This eventually led to a British show of force with warships, which caused King Kamehameha III to cede the sovereignty of the Kingdom of Hawai'i to Great Britain in 1843. Interestingly, this action was reversed by British Rear Admiral Richard Thomas when he, based on his understanding of British foreign policy, took down the British flag and proclaimed the sovereignty of the Hawaiian Islands back under the control of the king of Hawai'i. Other military incursions continued throughout the years. One other instance involved French sailors landing and destroying large parts of the Honolulu fort in 1849.

The Decline of the Kingdom of Hawai'i

King Kamehameha III died not too long after the Great Mahele, on December 14th, 1854. This led to disputes over who should inherit his lands and titles. Eventually, matters were settled in accordance with King Kamehameha III's wishes, and his adopted son, Alexander Liholiho (not to be confused with King Kamehameha II, whose birth name was Liholiho), was to become the successor to the throne. He was proclaimed King Kamehameha IV by his biological father, Mataio Kekuanao'a, who was the governor of O'ahu. Tragically, King Kamehameha IV's rule was cut short by his unexpected and premature passing. His rule lasted only nine years.

Frontal portrait of King Kamehameha IV, Alexander Liholiho. (Source: Leopold Grozelier)

He had suffered from chronic asthma for quite some time and was also deeply in grief over the death of his four-year-old son, Prince Albert, in 1862. These events proved to be too great for Alexander Liholiho; he passed away at the young age of twenty-nine. Then, a council consisting of the members of the Hawaiian Cabinet and other advisors to the king decided that because there was no heir to the throne, Prince Lot Kapuaiwa, the older brother of the late King Kamehameha IV, was to become king. He would go on to become King Kamehameha V. However, because of Alexander Liholiho's sudden death and lack of political preparation, many factions did not see Prince Lot's ascension as legitimate, especially since there was no joint ballot undertaken with the House of Nobles and the House of Representatives, which were major players in Hawai'i's political sphere. In spite of these objections, Victoria Kamamalu, sister to both Prince Lot and Alexander Liholiho, was rightly instituted as the queen regent (*Kuhina Nui*). And under Article 47 of the 1852 Constitution of the Kingdom of Hawai'i, she was well within her powers to name a successor to the throne in the absence of the king. She named Lot.

In a strange course of fate, King Kamehameha V also reigned for only nine years, passing away on December 11th, 1872, at the age of forty-two. Yet again, a named successor was not available to ascend the throne, and this caused some amount of confusion and consternation. During this time, William Charles Lunalilo emerged as a favorite for the throne, as he had attended the Royal School, which was run by American missionaries. William Lunalilo was also a descendant of Kalaimamahu, who was the half-brother of King Kamehameha I. He was chosen by an overwhelming majority of a collection of male electorates and was soon confirmed as the successor to the throne by the legislature of Hawai'i. Again, as ill fate would have it, Lunalilo would become king, only to pass away a little over a year later due to complications of tuberculosis and other related ailments.

Nevertheless, during his short reign, King Lunalilo enacted laws that would change the course of Hawai'i's history forever. In a move that was considered very divisive, King Lunalilo offered to exchange the lagoon of Pearl Harbor to the United States in exchange for the exemption of taxes on a number of Hawaiian goods that were exported to the United States, mainly sugar. However, the king withdrew the offer before it was deemed official due to significant pushback from the other *ali'i* and the general public. This event showed that the people and rulers of Hawai'i harbored deep feelings of distrust, bitterness, and suspicion toward foreign involvement and land treaties. Additionally, King Lunalilo behaved contrary to King Kamehameha V's example by electing three American ministers to seats of power and by cooperating and associating himself with the missionaries.

After King Lunalilo's death in 1874, the updated Constitution of 1864 assigned the task of choosing an heir to the Cabinet Council along with the Legislative Assembly. The two main royals that were considered were Queen Emma, who was the widow of King Kamehameha IV, and David Kalakaua, a descendant of a high-ranking *ali'i* who hailed from Hilo. Both David Kalakaua and Queen Emma were passionately patriotic and wanted to help preserve the royal line and the Kingdom of Hawai'i. A divide between the foreign powers' support for each of these royals began to form, with British interests aligning more with Queen Emma and American interests aligning more with David Kalakaua. Eventually, the legislature elected David Kalakaua, and this ended the Kamehameha era of the Kingdom of Hawai'i.

King David Kalakaua, circa 1870s. (Source: Hawai'i State Archives, photograph by Menzies Dickson)

King Kalakaua's ascension to the throne started the Keawe-a-Heulu royal line and saw a time of growing American influence on the Hawaiian Islands. Even though David Kalakaua was advised against going forward with the Reciprocity Treaty, he negotiated with the Americans and eventually ratified the bill in 1875. This treaty essentially allowed free trade between Hawai'i and the United States, but more importantly, it did not sign over any Hawaiian land to the Americans. However, many legislators and businessmen suspected that this would give the United States economic leverage over Hawai'i and eventually lead to American annexation (an illegal administrative conquest backed by force) of the area of Pu'u Loa, which would later be called Pearl Harbor.

Afterward, foreign interests and plantation companies dearly wanted to invest more resources into the sugar plantations of Hawai'i and especially buy more land. However, they were barred from doing so. King Kamehameha V had passed an act in 1865 that prohibited any alienation of the crown lands. The economic boom was immense and pushed the Western-run press to consistently publish and promote propaganda and articles that were in favor of selling more land, stating that allowing such transactions to take place would benefit all, no matter their class. Many foreign investors, spokespeople, businessmen, and newspapers repeated the view that more sales of land would lead to an influx of revenue in Hawai'i and enable both the royal family and the nation at large to benefit and prosper, enjoying a more secure, modern, and higher quality of life.

Eight years into his reign as king, David Kalakaua would turn against the United States' interests and seek a more independent path for the Kingdom of Hawai'i. This move would ultimately lead to the Bayonet Constitution being forced on Kalakaua in 1887 and the overthrowing of the Kingdom of Hawai'i.

The Bayonet Constitution and the Overthrow of the Kingdom of Hawai'i

The Hawaiian kingdom effectively ended in 1893 with a violent seizure of power from Queen Lili'uokalani, which was backed by the United States Marines. Before this, most of the crown lands were maintained in a relatively unchanging and productive manner by their commissioners. There were a number of factors and preceding events that led to the end of the Kingdom of Hawai'i, much of which is intimately connected with the United States of America.

One of the more impactful pieces of legislation that was passed was the 1874 Nonjudicial Mortgage Act, which effectively allowed a lender to auction off the borrower's land deed in the event that the mortgagee had fallen behind in payments. This auction could be carried out without any judicial oversight and resulted in many *Kuleanas* (land titles and rights from the Kuleana Act of 1850) passing from native hands to foreign ones. Moreover, the phenomenon of "adverse possession" also meant that many natives lost their lands to sugar plantation corporations. Adverse possession meant that if a party utilized a part of the land against the interests of the land's legal owner for an extended period of time, the land could be obtained from its original owner. The problem was that the time period for adverse possession to take effect was unusually short in regards to Native Hawaiian land, being only five years long. During this time, King Kalakaua worked closely with the Americans to promote the development of sugar plantations to secure Hawai'i's future. The collapse of some whaling fleets in the north and less traffic to the Hawaiian Islands were also impetuses for Hawai'i to find and develop its own resources. All in all, the number of sugar plantations in Hawai'i increased from twenty to over sixty in just five years. After David Kalakaua turned against American interests and began focusing on Hawaiian nationalism, a secret organization called the Hawaiian League began working to institute a new government in the Hawaiian Islands by any means necessary. The members of this organization were almost all Caucasians, and they also played major roles in the overthrow of the kingdom in 1893. Upon uniting with the Honolulu Rifles, an all-Caucasian civil militia, they outmaneuvered King Kalakaua and gained control of the city. King Kalakaua called on the ministers of Britain, France, Japan, and Portugal for help and even offered to hand over the Kingdom of Hawai'i in exchange for protection and control, but they refused to intervene.

The Hui Aloha ʻAina o Na Kane, or the Hawaiian Patriotic League for Men, who would petition against the eventual annexation, circa 1893. (Source: Library of Congress)

Severely outgunned and under threat of assassination, King Kalakaua was forced to accept a new Cabinet and complete the new Constitution of 1887, which would eponymously become known as the Bayonet Constitution, as it was signed under duress. Shortly after this, Pearl Harbor began to be militarized and developed as a naval base for the United States. After the Bayonet Constitution was imposed upon him, King Kalakaua continued his duties, even though the limitations of the new constitution frustrated his people and brought about staunch and vocal opposition. Men had to meet certain conditions before they could vote, and the actions of the king had to be approved by the Cabinet, which included a number of foreigners. Debates were had about whether the handing over of Pearl Harbor to the United States would help prevent annexation or further embolden foreign powers.

David Kalakaua passed away in 1891 while he was traveling to Washington to meet with Hawaiian ambassador Henry Carter to discuss the 1890 McKinley Tariff, which would nullify most of the free trade agreements of the previously signed Reciprocity Treaty. He was succeeded by his sister, Liliʻuokalani, who had already served as queen regent during one of

King Kalakaua's earlier trips. She continued her brother's fight to preserve the independent Kingdom of Hawai'i but was ultimately overthrown. She, too, fought to dismiss the reforms and revisions that were driven by the 1887 Bayonet Constitution, writing that the 1887 Constitution had been imposed by "aliens determined to coerce my brother."

Upon her becoming the queen, Queen Lili'uokalani received well over six thousand petitions and letters from all over Hawai'i, urging her to create a new constitution. This was an impressive number since it was more than two-thirds of the 9,500 or so registered voters of the land. Scholars and community leaders have estimated it to be very close to the entire population of native-born and half-native people. Such a new constitution would have allowed Hawai'i great power over its own authority and autonomy, allowing the monarch to appoint and remove members of the Cabinet and limit voter rights to naturalized and Native Hawaiians, removing much of the voting block of temporary residents.

A digitally colored and restored work of a photograph of Queen Lili'uokalani, circa 1887. (Source: Digitally reworked by Mark James Miller, original photograph by Walery, London, from the Hawai'i State Archives)

Some members of the queen's Cabinet had refused to sign her newly proposed constitution, and this was an opportunity for a small group called the Annexation Club to begin movements toward the annexation of Hawai'i by the United States of America. The overthrow was essentially led by a number of American businessmen who had become immensely wealthy from Hawai'i's sugar plantations. After a long period of planning and laying the political and legislative framework before hostilities ensued, these men won the support of the United States of America. On January

16th, 1893, the main coordinating American political representative, John Leavitt Stevens, effectively secured the island of Oahu with approximately 162 armed soldiers. They placed Queen Liliʻuokalani under house arrest. The military presence of the warship USS *Boston* also helped secure American buildings like the US Consulate and Arion Hall.

It was only in 1993, one hundred years after the overthrow, that the United States Congress acknowledged and admitted to the fact that US military and diplomatic officials had played an essential role in facilitating the overthrow of the Kingdom of Hawaiʻi. The power vacuum that was left was temporarily filled by the Provisional Government of Hawaii, which consisted of the coup leaders. After approximately a year and a half, the Provisional Government of Hawaii gave way to the Republic of Hawaii, which was a sovereign state that was not officially a part of the United States until 1898, even though the Republic of Hawaii had the military and political support of the United States. This meant that the Republic of Hawaii only lasted for about four years. The overthrow was an illegal act that went against international laws and is considered a black mark on the history of the United States of America, even though it issued a formal apology for such activities.

A photograph of US Marines and sailors from the USS Boston occupying Arlington Hotel grounds during the overthrow of Queen Liliʻuokalani, 1893. (Source: Hawaiʻi State Archives)

Land of Sugar

The incredibly fertile lands and stable, warm climate of Hawaiʻi proved to be ideal for the growth of sugarcane, which would eventually lead to the dominance of sugarcane over Hawaiian agriculture and sugar exports' iron-clad hold on the Hawaiian economy and overseas interests. Beginning in the 1820s onward, sugar plantations cropped up on the islands of Oʻahu, Maui, Kauaʻi, Molokaʻi, Lanaʻi, and the Big Island of Hawaiʻi itself. Over the next one hundred years, sugar production from Hawaiʻi would grow from under fifty thousand tons of sugarcane to well over half a million tons.

This had several effects. The first was a huge influx of immigrant labor to help cope with the demands of a rising sector, especially since growing, harvesting, and processing sugarcane was a labor-intensive process. Tens of thousands of laborers were contracted from Japan, China, the Philippines, Puerto Rico, and Korea. Hawai'i's population swelled by over 300,000 people over this time and resulted in the percentage of Native Hawaiians dropping to about 10 percent of the total population by the 1900s. It was said that a good tradesman could depend on being gifted some land, along with a native wife, if he was productive and stayed. Sanford Dole, whose relatives would eventually found the Dole Food Company we know today, also wrote and supported the need to increase Hawai'i's population, whether by increasing the flow and residency of immigrant labor or by encouraging current residents to have large families. His view was that the islands would never reach their full productive power without occupying them to a much greater extent.

A photograph of Chinese contract laborers working on a sugar plantation, circa the late *1900s. (Source:* Hawaiian Journal of History, *Vol 23, 1989, article: "Chinese in Hawai'i: A Historical and Demographic Perspective"* by Eleanor C. Nordyke and Richard K. C. Lee)

During the early 1920s, the Hawaiian Sugar Planters' Association's recruiters would examine the hands of Filipinos who wanted to work with them; only those with the distinct hardened and callused palms of farm and field workers would be accepted.

Filipino workers would come to work on Hawai'i's sugarcane fields, dairy industries, and sugar mills. Some of them would work for over thirty years, eventually retiring and settling in Hawai'i as permanent residents. Workers would often be seen as lesser by Caucasian business-owners, especially if they were of obviously different ethnic backgrounds. Some plantation owners and foremen would call workers out by their identification numbers, even though some of them would protest and ask to be called by their names.

A bronze sculpture of various plantation workers at the Old Sugar Mill Monument, Kaua'i, *Hawai'i, a work done by Jan Gordon Fisher. (Source: Wikimedia Commons, Joel Bradshaw)*

Significant environmental degradation and pollution also resulted from the proliferation of sugarcane plantations. The islands suffered not only from the pollution of coal-burning and iron smelting but also from deforestation due to a ravenous need for both timber and wood fuel. All of this was further exacerbated by a relative lack of fresh water on the islands, as oceanderived water sources contain salt. Owing to the fact that sugarcane is a crop that requires an immense amount of water to grow and farm, the plantation boom led to forests being cleared and tunnels being constructed to aid in freshwater procurement. Water catchment areas in the mountains were diverted toward the plantations, and deep wells were dug. Even with improvements in technology and efficiency, it took over one ton of water to produce one pound of refined sugar.

Many American businessmen would seize the chance to buy and invest in Hawaiian lands for the purposes of setting up sugar or pineapple plantations. Californian sugar magnate Claus Spreckels came to Hawai'i in 1876 and negotiated a very controversial and tenuous deal with Princess Ruth Ke'elikolani, a descendant of the Kamehameha line. This allowed him to acquire thousands of acres of land. Another famous and notable American that would contribute heavily toward the Westernization of the Hawaiian Islands was Sanford Dole, who would serve as the only president of the Republic of Hawaii. Sanford was raised in Protestant missionary schools, and his father was the principal at what would eventually come to be known as the Punahou School. He was appointed as a justice in the Supreme Court of the Kingdom of Hawai'i by King Kalakaua, and his cousin, James Dole, would eventually come to Hawai'i to found the Hawaiian Pineapple Company. This company would later become the Dole Food Company, which is well known even today.

Brochure by the Hawaiian Pineapple Packers' Association, Honolulu, Hawai'i, 1914. (Source: Hawaiian Pineapple Packers' Association)

The United States and Hawai'i actually had an amicable and mutually beneficial relationship leading up to the 1890s. It had established several treaties with the United States that fostered political goodwill and ensured commercial and navigational cooperation between the two nations. Further, President John Tyler had also issued an official statement in 1842 that included Hawai'i under the Monroe Doctrine, which proclaimed certain acts of European colonialism as a potential act of hostility toward the United States. This meant that the USA recognized the independent existence of Hawai'i and that they would oppose an invasion of the islands by any other power.

In the end, the annexation goal was spurred on by falling sugar prices and the rising belief that the United States must control Hawai'i against other foreign interests and to protect the West Coast of the contiguous United States of America. There was also a perceived air of economic instability and the potential for an economic depression to beset the islands. This spurred Americans like Lorrin Thurston and Minister John L. Stevens to zealously promote and push the idea of annexation abroad, leading to many US politicians to buy into the idea. Stevens asked the US State Department to send additional naval forces to protect American interests and asked Washington to station a warship in Honolulu indefinitely to secure the islands. This was the beginning of a rapid increase in American military might in Hawaiʻi.

Chapter 7 – World War II and Hawai'i

Hawai'i's role in World War II is complex, deep, and pivotal. Most importantly, the geographic location of the islands of Hawai'i meant that they were both a target of and a boon to whichever superpower of WWII controlled it. Many battles of the Pacific Ocean would later be launched from, headquartered by, and supported through the islands of Hawai'i.

Prior to Hawai'i's contact with the "outside world," its economy was self-sustaining and almost self-contained. After its existence was popularized to the outside world, the Hawaiian Islands' economy underwent a change, as it became the treasured stop at which whalers, fishermen, and voyagers stopped to refuel, restock, and rest. The established history of the usefulness of the islands made it famous around the world and also added to its importance in determining control of the Pacific Ocean. Additionally, the familiarity of the waters, winds, threats, and routes that surrounded the Hawaiian archipelago further increased its international visibility and recognition. Over time, its economy changed to become agricultural, thus supplying the United States of America and other foreign powers with precious produce and goods. This led to

Hawai'i playing more and more into the hands of American political interests, and it eventually became the turning point of the Pacific Ocean conflict.

Suffice to say, Pacific supremacy could not possibly be attained by a large political superpower without some kind of footing in the Polynesian chain, and Hawai'i was at its center. As we've seen from the previous chapter, due to its contact with the United States, the largely isolated archipelago of Hawai'i was transformed slowly but surely into an outpost of the United States, with a focus on the eventual need for military capabilities. Add to the mix the preestablished sugar plantations and vested interests of the markets of the United States of America, and it should come as no surprise that Hawai'i was targeted by the Japanese, eventually leading to the infamous attack on Pearl Harbor.

Caught in between Japan and America

The historical centrality of Hawai'i for Pacific travelers meant that it had long-established relationships with fur traders, whalers, sandalwood traders, and merchants from China, the Americas, and even Europe. Then, mostly due to its availability of fertile land, temperate and suitable climate, influx and abundance of Asian laborers, and the arrival of opportunistic American businessmen, Hawai'i became an immensely productive and popular exporter of sugar, not only for the American market but also for Japan. By the mid-19th century, Hawai'i's location and function in the Pacific simultaneously put it at the crossroads of two global superpowers and made it the most strategic chain of islands to control.

The twenty-year period of tenuous global peace between WWI and WWII saw US-Japan relations slowly worsen, even though the two nations were reasonably amicable to begin with. A series of historical events gradually soured diplomatic relations. In 1924, America placed a quota on Japanese immigration, which included the islands of Hawai'i, and the Great Depression of the 1930s made matters much worse. At the height of tensions, many business leaders, academics, and regional and religious leaders came together to form the Institute of Pacific Relations (IPR), which was conceived as an unofficial attempt to join countries along the Pacific Rim in a cooperative stance and foster the increasingly important idea of a "Pacific Community." A good number of Americans joined, and the idea garnered some support from the surrounding nations, such as the Philippines, Korea, Japan, China, New Zealand, and Canada. Naturally, the organization chose to host its international conference in Honolulu in 1925 to discuss its issues and concerns. Although the IPR eventually dissolved and failed to prevent conflict in the region, it remains a clear and documented case of international interests being aligned to view Hawai'i not merely as a keystone of naval dominance but also of its prospects and potential for economic cooperation.

Eastern Problems for America's West Coast

For a long time, the United States of America focused much of its security concerns on the Atlantic Ocean and the Caribbean. The recognition of the Pacific Ocean as a vitally important front for war was not high on America's list of priorities. Only after Japan's attack on Pearl Harbor did the strategic significance of Hawai'i become a top priority, so much so that the current headquarters for the commander in chief of the US Pacific Command is located in Hawai'i, and it is the central base for US Navy, Air Force, and Army operations for the region.

The buildup of the United States' interest in Hawai'i as a strategic point of military power began with President Theodore Roosevelt and an advisor of his named Alfred Thayer Mahan. Considered one of the most important United States naval figures of the 19th century, one of Alfred Mahan's core influences on American military thought was the emphasis he placed on the significance of the Pacific Ocean for US security. Nowadays, most of his strategic thinking and writings are collectively referred to as "Mahanism," and it typically places great importance on naval power. This would eventually lead to him lending his voice to and arguing in favor of the US annexing Hawai'i, which occurred in 1898. Specifically, the threat of Japan to the US was the key factor in the thinking that placed such military importance on Hawai'i. Along with other popular writers, Mahan wrote about other concerns, such as the Japanese immigrants failing to assimilate with the culture of the United States. These writings both directly and indirectly fueled hysteria around the sensational image of the "Yellow Peril," a racist ideology that targeted people of East Asian descent. This hysteria would eventually bleed over to the islands of Hawai'i, which was home to a large and growing population of Japanese migrant workers.

Photograph of Alfred Thayer Mahan, circa 1897. (Source: The Bookman, An Illustrated Literary Journal, Volume V)

A mere ten years after the US annexed Hawai'i, construction of a fully-fledged naval base began in Pearl Harbor. During Theodore Roosevelt's presidency, which lasted from 1901 to 1909, he asked for Pearl Harbor to be fortified, and the United States Congress agreed. However, the process was both slow and inadequate, as most US Navy officials and politicians did not share similar worries over the Pacific theater of war. The number of men stationed in Hawai'i saw a sharp increase to over twelve thousand personnel during the First World War but decreased to just below five thousand men afterward.

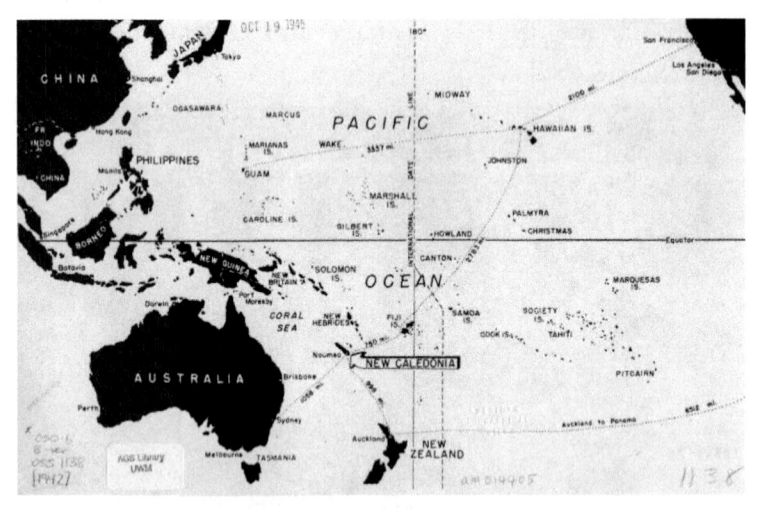

A 1942 map of the Pacific Ocean, with Los Angeles in the upper right connected to the Hawaiian Islands and Guam, along with Japan situated in the upper left. (Source: Central Intelligence Agency, Washington)

The Japanese invasion of Manchuria in 1931 triggered a renewal of forces in Hawai'i. This happened again when the Empire of Japan waged an undeclared war against China in 1937. Signs of impending war with Japan were looming, and all sorts of pressures were building up to an eventual outbreak of conflict. Such pressures would be materially reflected in the lives of Hawaiians as well, including annual blackout drills and exercises for Hawaiian civilians in Honolulu. Civil defense units and outposts began to spring up in rural areas and surrounding military installations. Further, emergency disaster preparations began in 1940, with Honolulu women being tasked with surgical dressing and wound bandage production. There were also first-aid training sessions held by the local Red Cross. Honolulu saw the establishment of a blood bank, and the city's Schofield Barracks would grow to become one of the largest US Army installations in the world, hosting and fielding over forty thousand troops by 1941. The primary objective of such a large force was to hold and defend Pearl Harbor and, by extension, Hawai'i from Japanese raiders and invaders. Incidents like the bombing of the SS *President Hoover*, the flagship *Augusta*, and the sinking of the USS *Panay* were strong indicators that Hawai'i was going to be sandwiched between two political and military bulldozers.

Pearl Harbor

On December 7th, 1941, Japan launched an attack called the "Hawaii Operation" on the US naval base of Pearl Harbor, Honolulu. Japan intended to cripple the United States' ability to utilize its naval fleet in the Pacific Ocean, as it could potentially interfere with Japan's military maneuvers in Southeast Asia. It is important to note that the attack on Pearl Harbor was but one instance in a coordinated chain of nearly simultaneous attacks planned and executed by the Empire of Japan. Some of these attacks included Japan's invasion of British Malaya (modernday Malaysia), the invasion of Hong Kong from the north, and the invasion of Batan Island, which was Japan's first foray into the Philippines. Unbeknownst to Hawai'i, the US military actually intended to withdraw from the Philippines in the event of an invasion. This withdrawal did indeed happen once the Empire of Japan made its intentions clear with its move on Pearl Harbor, and although Pearl Harbor was the second attack the Japanese made, being half an hour or so behind the invasion of Kota Bharu (the start of the invasion of British Malaya), it was by far the most important and impactful point of attack.

The attack came out of nowhere, and the morning of December 7th can only be described as a scene of utter chaos and confusion. Japan had not declared war on the US, and by all accounts (except for conspiracy theorists), the attack was a complete surprise. Hundreds of Japanese planes bombed and shot the naval base of Pearl Harbor, killing many people and destroying many ships. The ferocity of the battle is well-documented and paints a horrific experience. Oral and eyewitness accounts of Pearl Harbor say that, at first, natives and other residents of Oʻahu thought it was merely some form of routine firing practice, as gunshots were something that people heard often. It wasn't until a superintendent or another person in charge came running while bearing the sobering news that people began to scatter, either to help the defense effort, seek shelter, or warn others. The attack lasted for about an hour and twenty minutes.

A photograph taken just as the USS Shaw, a destroyer ship, exploded from the Japanese attack on Pearl Harbor, December 7th, 1941. (Source: US archives, unknown Navy photographer)

Ultimately, the United States suffered heavy losses in the aftermath of the attack, losing multiple battleships, cruisers, destroyers, and aircraft. US casualties numbered well over two thousand soldiers, sailors, Marines, and civilians. Huge swaths of the docks and many hangars and buildings were either destroyed or damaged. In fact, some of the damage to the buildings is visible even today. Furthermore, hundreds of American aircraft were lost to general-purpose and armor-piercing bombs dropped by Japanese planes, with the overwhelming majority of the aircraft being destroyed while on the ground and in hangars. Due to the chaotic nature of the ambush and the devastation unleashed by the Japanese, American Air Force pilots had immense difficulty in taking off during the attack to fight back. This effectively meant that Japanese planes had full reign over the skies.

A small boat goes to rescue seamen from the burning battleship, the USS West Virginia. Thick smoke chokes the air and water surface. (Source: Library of Congress, Prints and Photographs Division)

The Japanese forces, on the other hand, suffered very few losses. A few smaller submarines were destroyed, and twenty-nine planes were lost, along with sixty-four lives. The entire attack was carried out through two waves of attack planes launched from Japanese aircraft carriers. They had left Hitokappu Bay, which was located to the north of Japan, approximately two weeks prior to the attack. These aircraft carriers were huge ships that were large enough to carry, fuel, and deploy hundreds of fighter and bomber planes. The first Japanese wave was much more successful than the second wave, as the initial attack made the Americans realize they had to prepare and mount an anti-air defense strategy. Japanese torpedoes, bombs, armorpiercing bombs, and high-capacity automatic guns targeted US troops, battleships, aircraft, outposts, and bases to great effect. The attack marked the official entry of the United States of America into the Second World War.

For a long time, Japan's lack of an official declaration of war before launching the attack was portrayed and thought of by many scholars as late. This supposed lateness was thought to be caused by a number of factors, like the United States' inefficiency of diplomatic communications, its complicated bureaucracy, Tokyo's formal message of "peace negotiations were officially at an end" being too long, and other general factors of accidental bumbling and delays. However, the recent uncovering of official documents by Japanese scholar and professor Takeo Iguchi clearly shows that Japan did not comply with international law, as it purposefully and intentionally hid its true intention of war from the United States in hopes of succeeding in their surprise attack. Pearl Harbor was indeed planned and executed as a surprise attack, and its main objective was to cripple and neutralize the Pacific Fleet of the US Navy.

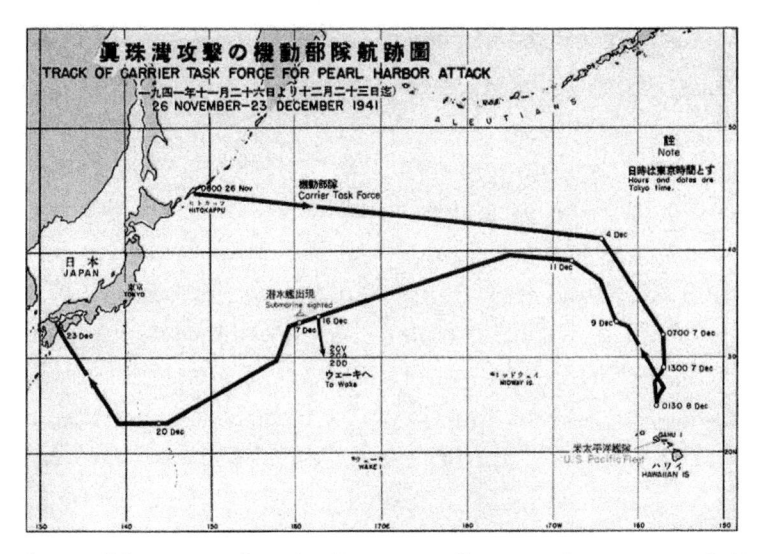

A chart of the route that the Japanese fleet used to approach Pearl Harbor. The arrows indicate their departure from the northern islands (Hitokappu Bay) to Hawai'i (bottom right) and then back to Japan. (Source: United States Army, Reports of General MacArthur, 1966)

Aftermath

The most important consequences of the attack on Pearl Harbor were that the United States of America formally entered the Second World War and declared war on Japan. The United States of America was considered to be a neutral player in the Second World War up to that point, as the country was officially bound by the Neutrality Acts that US Congress had passed. The acts were centered around isolationism and non-interventionism, making sure the US did not get involved in the two large conflicts that were going on in Europe and in Asia. On December 11th, 1941, Germany and Italy declared war on the United States of America, and US Congress issued declarations of war against Germany and Italy shortly after that. The attack on Pearl Harbor also united the people of America, with support for the war against Japan and its allies having well over 90 percent of the general public.

The Eastern Pacific had not yet seen a threat this global. The previous conflicts between groups of Hawaiians, the War of 1812, the Mexican-American War, the Chinese-Japanese War, the Japanese-Russian War, and even the First World War had all left impressions on the region but never so directly. Hawai'i was quickly strengthened and fortified by forces and resources sent by the United States. More importantly, the Japanese force had considered their tactical victory of destroying and crippling the American battleships and aircraft to be more complete than it actually was. Accordingly, the Japanese forces did not elect to target Pearl Harbor's navy repair yards, oil reservoirs, fuel storage hangars, submarine docks, dry docks, and headquarter buildings. These facilities proved to be more important to America's Pacific war effort than any ship, allowing the United States to provide logistical support to all of the US Navy's operations through Pearl Harbor.

In Hawai'i, however, the consequences were far quicker to materialize and involved changes to both the structure of daily life and to the demographics of the islands. Concerns about the loyalties of foreign and native-born Japanese people and other suspects were rounded up by military and FBI (Federal Bureau of Investigation) agents. The islands were placed under martial law, and a strict curfew was put into place. Late-night activities were limited due to a military-enforced curfew. These times were scary and stressful for all those living on the islands. Almost all of the islands' inhabitants were subjected to fingerprinting and issued personal papers and identifying documents. Even then, workers and residents with a night pass would sometimes be stopped and subjected to further scrutiny, as soldiers often had difficulty in telling Japanese people apart from Chinese, Filipinos, Koreans, or even Native Hawaiians. Many coastal areas were designated off-limits to the public, and guards were stationed on important shores, beaches, and cliffs.

Early Japanese immigrants that arrived in Hawai'i, 19^{h} century. (Source: Wikimedia Commons, hawaiihistory.org)

After the United States of America declared war on the Empire of Japan, it placed over 100,000 Japanese residents in internment camps for fear of misplaced loyalties. This eventually spilled over to Hawai'i, and although the great majority of people of Japanese descent were not shipped off to the internment camps on the mainland, such shipments still happened. Due to the prevalent fear of racial lines being drawn in the war and the threat of the "Yellow Peril," strategies of how to handle Hawai'i's population of Japanese people had to be devised. These plans involved taking certain "strategic hostages" and eventually registered and consigned Japanese people to live in isolated communities. Hawai'i had too many Japanese Americans and Japanese people to merit shipping all of them back to the mainland, and the island was in dire need of labor and expertise. Therefore, Hawai'i was slowly transformed into an internment camp of sorts, with watchful guards, gated communities, and strict laws being enacted. Employment opportunities for women increased dramatically in Hawai'i, as well as in many other parts of the world, as a result of World War II, with job openings for clerks, teachers, nurses, storekeepers, and even mechanics. Men were mostly wanted for physical labor and the war effort, but there was a major emphasis placed on the fact that agricultural work had to continue in spite of war. In fact, there are reliable accounts of plantation workers being refused enlistment because the government knew that the work they were doing in sugar mills and fields was more important to the war effort. Instead, some of the workers were assigned to "home guard" duty and given military ranks, training, and weapons. These men would be attached to the 21st Infantry of the United States Army, but most of them would never be shipped out. Workers would also "bleed" into the surrounding jobs, such as working in the plantation's hospital, assisting in the morgue, helping out with office and administrative duties, and working in foodservice. Hawai'i itself would not see any more attacks or battles for the remainder of World War II, and it was governed through the war with a military government, which was led by three military governors: Walter Short, Delos Emmons, and Robert Richardson Jr.

A call for nurses and nurse's aides from the Office of Emergency Management, dated between 1941 and 1945. (Source: US National Archives and Records Administration)

Chapter 8 – Modern Hawai'i

Hawai'i was considered a territory of the United States throughout the Second World War, and most, if not all, aspects of its governance were determined by a military government. Food and fuel were rationed, with priority given to the defenders, watch guards, soldiers, and sailors. Television, radio, and newspapers were censored, edited, and controlled by the Americans to stop enemy propaganda from spreading to the Hawaiian people. Trade, markets, and businesses were sometimes nationalized and, at other times, controlled and regulated to aid the war effort. Even courts, juries, and witnesses were beholden to the military effort, resulting in different American federal departments clashing over conflicting interests over the lands of Hawai'i as the Second World War raged on.

Political Transition

Before World War II, in 1900 to be specific, the United States Congress enacted the Hawaiian Organic Act, which was a piece of legislation that established the Territory of Hawaii and provided it with a constitution and governmental footing. As linguistic orthography was nowhere near as advanced back then as it is today, the more important American political documents have Hawai'i spelled as "Hawaii" without diacritics. Thus, the slight pause in the traditional Hawaiian pronunciation of the name is missing. (As you have noticed throughout the book, we have opted to use the traditional spelling unless Hawaiʻi is being used in a proper name, such as the State of Hawaii or the Republic of Hawaii.) The act would eventually be replaced by the Hawaii Admission Act in 1959, through which Hawaiʻi would gain statehood and join the United States of America as a state.

The martial law that had governed the islands of Hawaiʻi during the Second World War left a thirst for basic liberties in its wake. Toward the end of the war in 1944, as the Allied forces bolstered their hold on the Pacific theater, a transition out of martial law slowly took place. In an approximately two-year-long transitional phase, where extremely restrictive laws were progressively loosened, a movement toward a more democratic state of affairs began. Part of the driving force of this democratic movement was the realization and emphasis on the fact that Hawaiʻi had never voluntarily ceded political power to the United States of America and was, in effect, taken over by force.

The Republican Party of the United States had held power over the islands of Hawaiʻi since the Bayonet Constitution, and many sugar plantation oligarchs also retained vast amounts of land and political influence. In the face of rising racial tensions and awareness of discriminatory practices and policies, one particular politician would rise to the forefront and become the most influential politician in the affairs of Hawaiʻi for nearly two decades. That politician was John Anthony Burns, and his political legacy is undoubtedly significant. Among the American officials who came to govern Hawaiʻi, he is seen as a benevolent politician who, for the most part, had the interests of Hawaiʻi at heart and brought about many improvements and valuable changes to Hawaiʻi and her people.

John A. Burns, second governor of Hawaii, in his meeting with President Lyndon B. Johnson, February 6th, 1966. (Source: Public domain, Online Photo Archive Search)

John Burns was born in Montana and moved to Hawai'i in his early twenties, finding work as a police officer. When the war with Japan broke out, he was promoted to the head of the Honolulu Police Department's Espionage Bureau and tasked with vetting the Japanese population of Hawai'i. Through this assignment, John Burns would come to know the Japanese and Native Hawaiian communities very well, which proved helpful in shaping his later policies. By the end of World War II, Burns turned his eyes to a career as a politician, and he had a specific, revolutionary aim in mind. John Burns would build a political coalition that would eventually include many factions of people, including war veterans, labor unions, select members of the Communist Party of Hawaiʻi, and Japanese Hawaiians and Americans.

Amidst the many people who were racial and social elitists, John Burns was starkly different. He had suffered many tragedies and setbacks in life, and he pushed a new, progressive political front, one in which he sought to put an end to historical privilege as much as possible and give every citizen an equal opportunity to realize their dreams and aspirations. After about eight years, Hawaiʻi would undergo its Democratic Revolution of 1954, which was led by Burns himself, and he would go on to win Hawaiʻi's election for governor. Burns would go on to be reelected two more times in 1966 and 1970. John Burns was also elected as Hawaiʻi's delegate to Congress and is credited with many things, including spearheading the movement for Hawaiʻi's statehood, reinvigorating multiple economic sectors, and drastically improving and expanding Hawaiʻi's educational institutions. John Burns sadly passed away in 1973 after battling cancer. His death saw an outpouring of praise and adulation that had not been seen since the days of King Kalakaua himself.

The movement to break from the Territory of Hawaii came forward as a series of elections that pressured the existing Hawaii Republican Party. There were mass protests, general strikes, and acts of civil disobedience. Labor union strikes and the people's demands played a major role in defining the economic pressures that would allow the Hawaiian people to have more influence over their own political fate. Over time, these events would eat away and greatly diminish the power of sugarcane plantation corporations and the Big Five Oligopoly. The Big Five were five agricultural companies that mainly focused on sugarcane and fruit plantations, although nowadays, they have mostly diversified their companies.

Early organizations of this push against the oligarchs and established business hierarchy were kept as an underground movement in order to prevent it from being quickly crushed. As it gathered momentum, strikes were arranged and carried out, often along ethnic lines. Due to the disunity amongst ethnic groups, companies could sometimes hire a different ethnic camp to help fill labor gaps when their original laborers went on strike. Many different factions and political groups rose and fell, including the fall of more communist and far-left parties. The Democrats began to win many more territories than the Republicans, and the push for statehood began shortly after. Outside of John Burns's contribution, politically astute and educated Hawaiians came together under the banner of the Democratic Party and began fighting within the construct of the American two-party system. They had reasoned that true political power and sovereignty over their native lands were closed to them as long as Hawai‘i was a territory, and they fueled the push toward statehood.

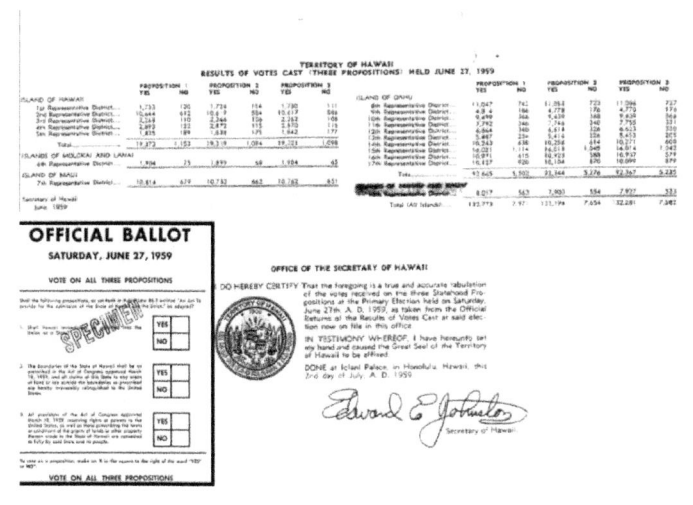

A composite image consisting of the results of the referendum (top), the official statehood vote ballot (bottom left), and the certification from Secretary of Hawaii Edward E. Johnston (bottom center). (Source: Public Domain, Wikimedia Commons, Grassroots Institute of Hawaii)

The push for statehood was not something new, even though it took a long time to finally achieve it. In the Treaty of Annexation of 1854, there is a clause expressing the early drafters' intentions to seek statehood at the earliest possible time. The political powers of Washington, DC, had shown little to no interest in giving Hawai'i statehood, and the opposition to Hawai'i's statehood used fears of communism as a mask to further their agenda. By 1956, good political maneuvering and coalition building had all but eliminated any communist concerns and brought many other issues to the forefront, making it strikingly harder to ignore the rising movement. Hawai'i's messenger, John Burns, arrived at Washington to find both the House and the Senate working with the Democratic majorities. Famously, John Burns brought and delivered the best of Hawaiian products like flowers, sugar products, and pineapples to congressional offices to help further his cause. After more vigorous lobbying, Congress passed the Admission Act, and a referendum was given to the Hawaiian people on whether to remain a US territory or to accept the new Hawaii Admission Act. The vote showed that 94 percent favored statehood. The Admission Act would be signed into law by President Dwight D. Eisenhower in 1959, admitting Hawai'i into the Union and making Hawai'i the most recent state to join the United States as of this writing.

The Second Hawaiian Renaissance

The First Hawaiian Renaissance is generally categorized as the initial push toward nationalism and revival of traditional Native Hawaiian customs, language, and practices. Scholars often quote this push as having started with King Kamehameha himself, but they also always specifically mention King Kalakaua, as he took significant steps to push Native Hawaiian culture into the modern age. An important instance of his steps to do so was when he replaced the Christian national anthem with "Hawai'i Pono'i," which remains its state song today. In particular, he commissioned the recording of hundreds of Hawaiian chants and recitations of myths and legends, such as the Kumulipo creation myth.

An official embraces the statue of King Kamehameha I during the lei-draping ceremony on King Kamehameha Day. (Source: Anthony Quintano)

The Second Hawaiian Renaissance was much more recent and was definitely driven from a musical perspective, which explains much of Israel Kamakawikoʻole's deep, influential legacy (his work will be discussed in the following chapter). The movement started in the late 1960s and saw a resurgence in Native Hawaiian music and Native Hawaiian artistry, along with a reinvigoration of local and academic interests in Hawaiian linguistics and language. Pidgin, also known as Creole, began to be studied and analyzed in earnest, as it bore incredibly important clues about linguistic universals and language creation. Additionally, other investigations and studies about traditional Native Hawaiian crafts and skills started gaining ground.

Naturally, Hawaiian literature and native-written poetry began gaining ground too, and they subsequently reinforced the Second Hawaiian Renaissance, as the literature often mentioned and explored the people of Hawaiʻi's past cultures and lost arts.

Fortunately, this movement also rediscovered and preserved the previous works of writers like David Malo, John Papa ʻIʻi, Kepelino, and Samuel Kamakau. This helped cement an understanding of old Native Hawaiian life and also spurred a generation of reconstructivist art like Hawaiian *kapa* (barkcloth tapestries), Hawaiian tattoos, feather capes, religious petroglyphs, and even hula itself. In fact,

Hawaiʻi became the first state in the United States of America to pass a law for "Percent for Art," in which large-scale projects and development plans needed to include a small percentage of space and funds for public art.

Forestry and land restoration efforts were also renewed, and places that were previously polluted or over-farmed began to be stewarded properly. This began in earnest on a federal level after the National Environmental Policy Act was passed in 1969, which was soon followed by similar laws being passed in different states. Then, work began on determining locations of critical habitats for endangered and threatened species and implementing recovery plans and advisory teams, much of which is continued to this day. Sadly, many Hawaiian forest birds, tree snails, and different plant life are already extinct, but encouragingly and unexpectedly, various different branches of the US military have incorporated environmental protection specialists into their personnel, and land preserves have been set aside on military bases for protecting and monitoring certain species.

Hawaiian arts, including the Hawaiian dance forms of hula, were brought back by Kalakaua's reforms and saw another resurgence with the Second Hawaiian Renaissance. Hollywood prominently featured hula, even though it was a commercialized and watered-down version of the dance, and it spread quickly through the Western world. Tourism spiked with the renewal of Native Hawaiian art forms. Hawaiian and resident artists like Herb Kawainui Kane, Keichi Kimura, Brook Kapukuniahi Parker, Hon

Chew Hee, and Ogura Yonesuke Itoh brought forth many beautiful and soulful Hawaiian depictions of sailing, ocean culture, native peoples, volcano landscapes, and many other facets of Hawai'i.

The Hawaiian Sovereignty Movement

More modern times have seen a resurgence in the movement for Hawai'i to regain more of its lost sovereignty, a grassroots movement that has been named the Hawaiian sovereignty movement. This push comes through many different lenses: economic, intellectual, political, historical, and social. In essence, the movement seeks some form of reparations or reformation from the United States of America due to the fact that Hawai'i was taken from its native rulers via illegal and forceful means. The issues that stem from Hawai'i being governed by the US have also added to the movement, citing problems like homelessness, lack of social mobility, real estate inflation, gentrification, poverty, and other issues that affect the islands of Hawai'i.

As Hawaiians regained their political and economic standing, the populace began to educate itself and organized to push back against the rulings of Washington, DC, due to the fact that federal regulations often did not sufficiently account for Hawaiian people and Hawai'i-specific problems. For example, even though the sugarcane and pineapple oligarchy had been largely neutered when compared to their golden days of power, many American magnates and businessmen still held sway over massive plots of land. These groups still had considerable monetary and political power and inevitably contributed to driving the urbanization and commercialization rates up past what Native Hawaiians could cope with. As the Hawaiian people regained their voice, it became more and more obvious to all onlookers that they should have more control over their own natural resources.

The Hawaiian flag, originally used in the days of the Kingdom of Hawai'i but turned upside down to symbolize Hawai'i's distress. This version of the flag is used by the Hawaiian sovereignty movement.

Part of the Hawaiian sovereignty movement that remains highly relevant today is the comparison between the rights of Native Americans and the rights of Native Hawaiians. Native Americans, along with Native Alaskans, possess constitutionally-enshrined rights to selfdetermination that Native Hawaiians largely do not. Although the US has, in modern times, recognized the rights and sovereignty of Native Hawaiians to mostly govern themselves and their islands, this recognition has not been made explicit. This lack of a clear-cut understanding and written legislation is a point of contention that continues even today, with many Hawaiian sovereignty groups fighting the US with awareness, protests, and the law.

Tourism and Commercialization

Tourism has become an important part of Hawai'i's economy, especially from the start of the 20th century onward. More recently, the market and awareness behind Hawai'i's tourism have matured, with more emphasis on responsible ecological tourism, proper native and historical representations, and genuine cultural experiences. With the United States Army having a large and significant presence on Hawai'i, transportation options were never an issue to people once tourism began taking off, with its roots being laid pre-World War II. Hawai'i was promoted as an exotic getaway that was still strongly American. The aesthetics of Hawai'i focused on flowers, sunlight, beaches, surfing, exotic dancers, and general tropical-paradise-themed elements. Although advertising the islands of Hawai'i as such undoubtedly drew many curious visitors, it painted a false narrative that would perpetuate itself through the decades to come.

Famous Hawaiian activist and author Haunani-Kay Trask wrote that even though many Americans had heard of Hawai'i, with some even having visited it, few knew of how Hawai'i came to be territorially incorporated and economically and politically subordinate to the United States. She goes on to remark that the vast system of capitalist tourism shows Hawai'i to millions of tourists every year but fails to show the true face of Hawai'i to any real percentage of those tourists. This pushback against the attitude of profit-centric tourism has slowly begun to gain recognition, making Hawai'i not just a fantasy getaway land that happens to be five hours from California by plane but an island nation with a rich history and diverse people.

Proponents and educators stress that such awareness is crucial for helping fight factually incorrect yet established stereotypes and misconceptions about Hawai'i and also prevent the further erosion and destruction of Native Hawaiian culture, historical artifacts, and land. For the past few decades, many business corporations and tourist industries have consistently pushed the case for more hotels, golf courses, and tourist-friendly showcases of cherry-picked facets of local culture. These campaigns often come at the cost of ecologically or historically important land, and they unavoidably increase real estate prices at artificial rates, resulting in gentrification. Nowadays, historians, activists, and scholars are utilizing modern technological platforms to reach out and show that

Hawai'i is much more than that. Ecological studies, educational institutions, and local organizations have played and will continue to play key roles in combating the watering down of Hawai'i as merely a vacation-destination island.

Chapter 9 – Notable People of Hawai'i

Akebono Taro

Chadwick Haheo Rowan is a Hawaiian athlete that began playing basketball as a center due to his immense height of six feet eight inches (203 centimeters) and his strength. He later went on to become Akebono Taro, the first non-Japanese-born sumo wrestler to attain *yokozuna* status, the highest rank in sumo.

For a brief period, he attended Hawaii Pacific University but flew to Japan when he was nineteen years old to start training in sumo at the Azumazeki stable ("stable" refers to a training house for sumo wrestlers). Chad Rowan then took on the *shikona* (sumo ring name) of Akebono, which means "new dawn" in Japanese.

His massive height, size, and strength soon made it obvious that he was a force to be reckoned with, rising rapidly through the sumo ranks. Upon reaching the top competitive division of sumo, he was awarded a special prize for defeating a *yokozuna*, a feat few beginner wrestlers ever manage to pull off. His impressive stature and size made him an instantly recognizable wrestler and helped boost the popularity of sumo overseas and within Japan. He, along with another incredibly famous Hawaiian sumo wrestler named Konishiki Yasokichi, were the pioneers in pushing foreign-born sumo wrestlers into the limelight. Konishiki would be the first non-Japanese sumo wrestler to reach the *ozeki* rank, but he would be denied a promotion to *yokozuna*.

Akebono's strong performances and championship wins in the 1990s eventually won him a *yokozuna* promotion. The rank of *yokozuna* is the highest possible rank of sumo champions, and it comes with special privileges and recognition. His reign as a *yokozuna* lasted eight long years and saw him win the championship eight more times, marking him as a strong contender and fan favorite. He became a Japanese citizen during this time.

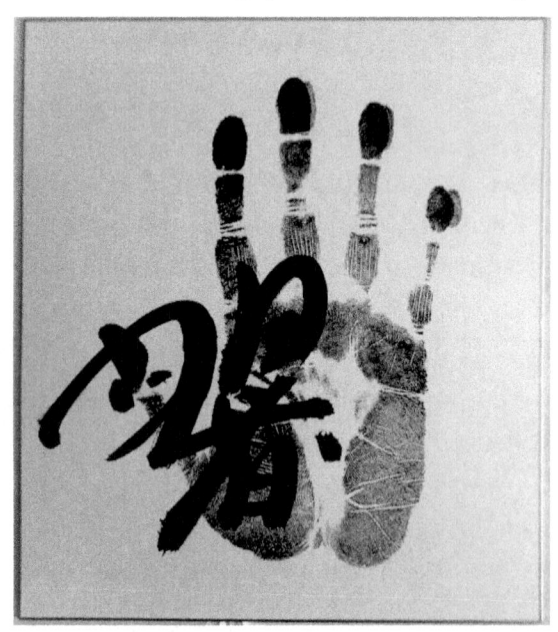

Official Tegata (handprint and signature) of Akebono Taro. (Source: Wikimedia Commons, Jeangigot)

Akebono's promotion was a groundbreaking moment in Japanese sumo, as it was once considered an unspoken rule that only Japanese-born wrestlers would be eligible for *yokozuna* status. The Yokozuna Deliberation Council had seen Akebono conduct himself with the dignity and humility necessary for such an exalted rank, even though they had previously turned down Konishiki for *yokozuna* promotion. Akebono's genuine passion for both the sport and the Japanese culture was obvious to many spectators, and he was even given the honor of representing Japan in the opening ceremony of the 1998 Winter Olympics after his fellow *yokozuna*, Takanohana Koji, fell ill.

Akebono's and Konishiki's contributions to the proliferation of Japanese sumo overseas and the gradual change in attitudes and perceptions toward non-Japanese wrestlers helped pave the way for many other *yokozuna* who were to come after them.

Barack Obama

Barack Obama was elected the forty-fourth president of the United States and served two terms from 2008 to 2016. He ran as a candidate for the Democratic Party and secured a win against his main opponents from the Republican Party, John McCain and Mitt Romney, respectively.

Both of Barack Obama's parents studied at the University of Hawaii and met each other there in 1960. They eventually got married on the island of Maui and had their only child together, Barack Obama. Obama was born on the island of Oʻahu in the capital city of Honolulu on August 4th, 1961. He spent most of his childhood years in Honolulu and was briefly brought back to Indonesia to visit his stepfather. Obama was schooled at Punahou School, a private school located in Honolulu. His life and upbringing were not religious, as his parents and grandparents were largely nonbelievers.

Obama then went on to study law at Columbia University and Harvard Law School. He is an accomplished lawyer, having taught constitutional law at the University of Chicago Law School for over ten years, becoming a senior lecturer. He also practiced law at the law firm of Davis, Miner, Barnhill & Galland, which specialized in civil rights litigation. There, he worked his way up the chain of seniority and ran a class-action lawsuit against Citibank Federal Savings Bank.

Obama is the first African American president of the United States and served both as a US senator and a state senator from Illinois before that. As the president of the United States, he signed many bills into law that were very impactful, even if the reforms themselves drew criticism. Some examples of these are the Affordable Care Act (also known as Obamacare), the 2009 American Recovery and Reinvestment Act, the Dodd-Frank Wall Street Reform and Consumer Protection Act, and many others.

Official photographic portrait of President Barack Obama. (Source: Pete Souza, 2009)

Many people cite Obama's presidency as a turning point for race relations in the United States of America. His stance on foreign matters was mixed, ranging from him overseeing the gradual withdrawal of US soldiers in Iraq to presiding over the mission that led to the death of Osama bin Laden. However, Obama also presided and defended PRISM, which was a code name for the program of mass surveillance that was carried out by the National Security Agency. Through this program, internet communications from various US internet companies were collected, stored, and monitored, supposedly for the safety of the American people. Although many portions of his presidential legacy have garnered harsh critiques, Barack Obama is still considered by scholars, political analysts, and historians to be a great president, and he enjoys a high level of popularity even today.

Barack Obama has written that living in Hawai'i allowed him to experience a wide variety of cultures and grow up in a climate of mutual respect. He quotes his mother as a shaping influence on his views, education, and exposure to the civil rights movement of the 1950s and 1960s, especially since the African American population was tiny, even in the ethnically diverse Hawai'i. His presidency has been and still is hailed as a watershed moment in American politics and another step in the correct direction of the American dream being available to all Americans.

Bruno Mars

Bruno Mars was born as Peter Gene Hernandez in Honolulu, Hawai'i, and quickly rose to international fame through his incredible vocal singing skills and wide range of flexible music styles. His work has included the genres of pop, rhythm and blues, funk, soul, rock, and reggae. Early on in life, he was exposed to a wide range of music styles, in particular the work of Elvis Presley. Bruno quotes Elvis and Michael Jackson as key inspirations for his onstage presence and performances. Growing up in Hawai'i and listening to the radio and his father's percussion performances, he was influenced by Hawaiian music and even hula music.

As a child, he was given the nickname Bruno, and later on, he decided to add Mars to make it sound like he was from another planet so that record labels and music companies would stop trying to pigeonhole him into being "the next Enrique Iglesias." His father is of Puerto Rican and Jewish descent, and his mother is Filipino and Spanish, and they met each other while performing in a show. Bruno would go on to become one of the best-selling music artists of all time, with well over 130 million records sold worldwide. He is known for a number of hit singles, including "Grenade," "When I Was Your Man," "Just the Way You Are," and "Uptown Funk." His fame, personality, philanthropy, and musical prowess have earned him multiple prestigious awards, including eleven Grammy Awards, nine American Music Awards, and three Guinness world records.

Bruno Mars, 2021. (Source: Wikimedia Commons, LXT Production)

After his parents divorced and his father's various businesses eventually failed, Bruno and his family had to move to the poorer neighborhoods of Hawai'i. He and his family grew up and worked their way through hard times, but Bruno holds fond memories of Hawai'i and regularly visits and holds concerts on the islands. He said that in the years when he was not yet famous, he would receive phone calls from home but remained evasive because he did not want to return to Hawai'i as a failure. He wanted to come back as a success and make his family and community proud of him. He credits much of his stage presence, techniques, and musical evolution to growing up in Hawai'i since he performed and helped out in a lot of shows with his father's band.

Even today, he remains a relevant and sought-after name in the music industry, recording features, remixes, and new albums that continue to break into the Billboard Hot 100. His ambiguous racial features have sometimes made him feel out of place in the music industry but have ultimately only boosted his popularity and appeal. This defiance of categorization has also flowed into his musical style, with retro elements pervading his music tours, diverse dance routines being showcased in his music videos, and unique music-genre fusions becoming typical for Bruno Mars over the years. He has done work centered around providing scholarships to Hawaiians who are venturing into the music industry through partnering with the Hawai'i Community Foundation and the Grammy Foundation. The program helps youths with training, careers, and interactive immersion, and it was established in honor of Bruno's mother.

Bethany Hamilton

Bethany Hamilton is a professional surfer who was born on the island of Kaua'i in 1990. She grew up in Hawai'i and was exposed to the sport of surfing very early on in her life, at the age of three. Most of Bethany's family were surfers too, and they helped nurture Bethany's newfound passion to greater heights. When she was only eight years old, she began to surf competitively, going on to eventually win first place in the 2002 Open Women's Division of the National Scholastic Surfing Association of the United States.

Bethany would go on to compete in many other surfing competitions and even win a good number of them.

On October 31st, 2003, while Bethany was going for a morning surf along the beaches and waves of Tunnels Beach, Kaua'i, she was attacked by a tiger shark that was over twelve feet long. The shark took a huge bite out of Bethany's surfboard and, at the same time, bit off Bethany's left arm. Bethany was lying on her stomach when the attack happened, and she was also talking to her fellow surfer and close friend, Alana Blanchard. The attack left Bethany in shock, and she was rushed to shore by Alana and Alana's brother and father. Bethany lost so much blood on the way to the hospital that she was passing in and out of consciousness. A doctor rushed to save her life and managed to stabilize her. The shark that was responsible for the attack was caught and killed by local fishermen. Undaunted, Bethany returned to surfing despite the extreme trauma of the incident, and she was riding the waves merely one month after the attack.

Bethany Hamilton crushing a wave in 2016. (Source: Wikimedia Commons, original photograph by Flickr user troy_williams)

The attack and Bethany's courage in the face of such a disaster received international coverage from various sources of media. She was invited as a guest onto numerous television shows, including *The Oprah Winfrey Show*, *Good Morning America*, and *The Ellen DeGeneres Show*. Furthermore, she was included in issues of *Time* magazine and *People* magazine with articles that mentioned her unflappable attitude and motivational story. Bethany is a devout Christian and has mentioned that the attack both tested and strengthened her faith in her religion, causing her to reevaluate her life and learn to appreciate every moment of it.

Bethany now has a custom-made board that is much easier to use and control with her right arm, and she continues to surf competitively. She has written several books about her experience, her life, and her faith, slowly developing a career as a motivational speaker and life coach. She has started and runs several outreach and charity programs, notably programs for women and men who have experienced tragic limb loss or amputees. These programs include a focus on cultivating a positive mindset toward life, fitness, and healthy living. Bethany is a mother of three and continues to inspire and educate women and men all over the world.

Duke Kahanamoku

Duke Kahanamoku, whose full name is Duke Paoa Kahinu Mokoe Hulikohola Kahanamoku, was born in 1890 in Honolulu, Oʻahu. His mother was a deeply religious woman, and he was named after his father, who was christened by a visiting bishop. Duke had an impressive stature, being over six feet tall and weighing nearly two hundred pounds. He boasted a physique that matched his athleticism. His build and his ability to conquer huge waves when surfing would earn him the nickname "The Big Kahuna," with *kahuna* meaning an expert. He would go on to work as a law enforcement officer, an actor, a surfboard designer and builder, a janitor, and also a businessman. However, his most famous achievements were in the Olympics, where he would become the first Hawaiian to win an Olympic medal.

Duke Kahanamoku surfing the waves of Waikiki, 1910. (Source: A.R. Gurrey, Jr.)

Duke was an incredible swimmer and surfer, and he went on to win the swimming gold medal for the 100-meter freestyle in the 1912 Summer Olympics that were held in Stockholm, along with a silver medal in the men's 4x200-meter freestyle relay race. He would win gold again in the 1920 Olympics and silver in the 1924 Olympics, effectively placing Hawaiian swimmers on the global map. Moreover, Duke Kahanamoku is widely credited with popularizing surfing and bringing it to Australia and California. His legacy gave the sport the kickstart it needed to become an international phenomenon and pastime, and he is honored with statues in California and Australia. Thanks to his contacts and popularity in California, he starred as a background actor and side character in many Hollywood movies as well. He mostly portrayed Native Hawaiian characters, fostering a new relationship between the shores of Hawai'i and California.

Heroically, in 1925, Duke rescued eight men from a fishing ship that had capsized due to heavy waves and rough seas off the coast of California's Newport Beach. Utilizing his surfboard, Duke swam back and forth from sea to shore, pulling people onto his board and helping them back to shore. This event was one of the many factors that ultimately led to surfboards becoming standard-issue equipment for lifeguards and water-rescue teams. Additionally, he lent his voice in support of Hawai'i's statehood movement and was elected the sheriff of Honolulu, a position he held for twenty-nine years.

Although he was discriminated against for his dark skin and complexion, he was never bitter or resentful. Instead, he carried an aura of confident optimism and calm joy, as noted by many people in their tributes of him after he passed in 1968 at the age of seventy-seven. To all scholars and historians of his life, it is clear that Duke Kahanamoku helped bridge the gap between the United States and Hawai'i. His ashes were scattered into the ocean.

Israel Kamakawiko'ole

Israel Kamakawiko'ole was a Hawaiian musician and singer who achieved international success for his songs and voice. Many music critics comment that Israel's music was quintessentially Hawaiian: simple yet deep and ad hoc in style and flow. Israel credits his uncle, Moe Keale, who was also a Hawaiian musician and ukulele maestro, for having a major influence on his music. An immense man, both literally and spiritually, Israel Kamakawiko'ole stood six feet two inches tall and weighed well over four hundred pounds. His music would grow to become a deeply inspirational, moving, and uniting force for Hawaiians around the world.

Israel, or Iz as he was affectionately and colloquially known, would be exposed to music from a very young age. Around the age of eleven, he would be invited on stage with his ukulele to perform and sing with Hawaiian musician Del Beazley, who noted that the first time he heard Iz perform, the whole room fell silent upon hearing him sing. Together with his older brother, Skippy Kamakawiko'ole, and a few other friends, Israel founded the

Makaha Sons, a band that would go on to become very famous and win awards in Hawai'i and overseas.

Unfortunately, Skippy died at the age of twenty-eight of a heart attack, an incident that was likely brought on by his obesity. Israel would go on to leave the band and start his journey as a solo musician, resulting in his first solo album being released in 1990. Afterward, what would become his most famous song, the medley "Somewhere Over the Rainbow/What a Wonderful World," would debut with his album *Facing Future* in 1993. *Facing Future* would go on to become Hawai'i's first-ever certified platinum album, selling over a million copies in the United States alone.

Israel Kamakawiko'ole, set against the scenic backdrop of Hawai'i. (Source: Wikimedia Commons, unknown)

Israel would go on to be awarded Male Vocalist of the Year, Favorite Entertainer of the Year, and Contemporary Album of the Year by the Hawai'i Academy of Recording Arts multiple times over his lifetime. He was known not only for his music; Israel also championed Native Hawaiian rights and independence, both through his lyrics and his words. Iz commented and touched on themes like social status, Native Hawaiian perceptions of themselves, drug abuse, and responsible parenting.

One of his last public appearances would become one of his most memorable and touching performances. In 1996, Israel would attend the Na Hoku Hanohano Award show and perform splendidly, despite being fed oxygen through a thin plastic tube due to his weight now being well over seven hundred pounds. Dressed in black and with sunglasses, Israel gave off an aura of cool composure and followed his song up by talking about his history with music, spreading love, connecting with native ancestry, and condemning drugs. Afterward, he would be pleasantly surprised by an onstage reunion with the Makaha Sons, describing his feelings as "I didn't know what was going on. I just had my eyes closed. I heard Moon's voice [Louis "Moon" Kauakahi] and I opened my eyes and looked to the side and there he was...I was crying, yeah, I was crying. There was a lotta emotions, a lotta feeling of love, an awesome feeling of aloha."

Tragically, the world-famous singer passed away at the young age of thirty-eight in 1997. Israel had struggled with obesity and obesity-related health issues from a very young age, as he absolutely loved starchy Hawaiian foods, although his genetics likely did not help. Diabetesrelated kidney and respiratory problems plagued him throughout the last years of his life, and his health was also further jeopardized by his earlier smoking and drug usage, which started when he was only fifteen. His marijuana usage gave him the "munchies," which further fueled his already large appetite.

Thousands of people attended his funeral at the Hawaii State Capitol to pay their last respects to an artist who was truly larger than life. People waited while standing for hours just to pass by his casket that was fashioned from the Koa tree, a massive tree endemic to Hawai'i. The Hawaiian flag flew at half-staff for the funeral of "The Voice of Hawai'i."

Chapter 10 – Culture of Hawai'i

Hawai'i is famous for many influences that now span the worldwide stage, which is an impressive achievement for the island nation. The products and offshoots of its culture are sometimes so renowned and representative of Hawai'i that it would be a travesty not to include them in this book.

Music and Dance

Ukulele

One of the aforementioned world-renowned Hawaiian objects is an instrument that is indeed world-famous, for it has been used and popularized by musical artists such as the aforementioned Israel Kamakawiko'ole, Taylor Swift, George Harrison of the Beatles, and more. Aside from appearing in countless talent show auditions, this instrument has gained popularity alongside the invention of plastics manufacturing and was exported all over the world. However, the ukulele is more than just a "smaller guitar"; it has been used not only as a symbol of Hawai'i's extensive and rich musical culture and history but also as a political tool, a tourist souvenir, or a sought-after collectible.

Hawaiian hula dancers with a guitar (center) and ukuleles (on either side). (Source: Hawai'i State Archives, original photograph by J.J. Williams)

In the 1920s, anthropologist and ethnomusicologist Helen Roberts was asked by Hawaiian officials to collect, record, and publish traditional and ancient songs, chants, and poems of the Hawaiian Islands. After over a year of work, she had compiled hundreds of records through interviews and trips. One of her most interesting findings was presented in a report that concluded the ukulele not to be of Hawaiian origin, even though it was (and still is) widely associated with Hawai'i by tourists, musicians, scholars, and even the Native Hawaiians. In truth, the ukulele descended from the Madeiran machete, with the word "machete" referring to an instrument, not a broad, heavy knife. It was introduced to Hawai'i by Portuguese immigrants from the island of Madeira, which is located off the coasts of Morocco and Portugal. The

Madeiran machete is an instrument that looks much like the ukulele; in other words, it looks like a small guitar. It is a string instrument that has five metal strings and is traditionally made of wood. This was the template upon which three carpenters would fashion the ukulele and claim to be the inventor of the instrument.

These three immigrant laborers were Manuel Nunes, Jose do Espirito Santo, and Augusto Dias, and they were all registered as cabinet-makers. Being carpenters, they had the necessary skills to begin fashioning a replica or variant of the Madeiran machete. Due to agricultural troubles in Madeira's wine industry around the 1840s, the island's economy took a turn for the worse. By the late 1870s, many people were desperate and destitute. Shortly after that, many of them left to look for better fortunes in a faraway place in the Pacific that was, at the time, called the Sandwich Islands. These islands were a six-month voyage away, but the workers—men and women both—were more than happy to take such a long trip for a chance at a better future. After their labor contracts expired, Nunes, Santo, and Dias went to Honolulu, the thriving city and commercial center of Hawai'i, and sought to make a living there. They all took up work and placed newspaper ads as guitar makers and furniture makers who dealt with stringed instruments and cabinets. Years later, they would each lay claim to being the inventor of the ukulele, but the truth is that they likely co-invented the instrument according to trends of economic demand and rising local popularity and, in the process, influenced each other.

MANUEL NUNES,
Manufacturer of
Guitars, Ukuleles,
TARO PATCH FIDDLES.
Workmanship and Material Guaranteed. Repairing a Specialty.
1130 :———No. 219½ KING ST.

An ad placed by Manuel Nunes in a Hawaiian newspaper, September 13[h], 1899. (Source: Wikimedia Commons, Hawai'i Digital Newspaper Project)

Jose de Espirito Santos

King street, - two doors below Punchbowl

MANUFACTURER OF

Guitars, : Ukuleles,

TARO PATCH FIDDLES.

Workmanship and material guaranteed. Repairing a specialty.

An ad placed by Jose do Espirito Santo in a Hawaiian newspaper, September 13th, 1899. (Source: Wikimedia Commons, Hawai'i Digital Newspaper Project)

A. DIAS,

Manufacturer of Ukuleles, Taropatch and Guitars.

All kinds of repair work.

1130 Union Street Honoulu.

An ad placed by Augusto Dias in a Hawaiian newspaper, January 10th, 1906. (Source: Wikimedia Commons, Hawai'i Digital Newspaper Project)

Nonetheless, the ukulele went on to sell millions of units made in different styles, especially in the USA. One of its charms was that it became a multimedia phenomenon, being played in nightclubs, restaurants, orchestras, and Hawaiian music groups. Mainstream artists of the time like Johnny Marvin, Ernest Ka'ai, and Frank Crumit soon picked the ukulele up and rode the instrument's popularity wave while simultaneously adding to it. The instrument even made it onto Broadway in the musical *Lady, Be Good*. Its spread even had *The New York Times* reporting that Edward, Prince of Wales, had expressed a desire to learn to play the instrument. Further Western coverage of music produced by the ukulele found its unique sound and timbre hard to describe, as it was decidedly different from the machete and the guitar.

In 1922, Manuel Nunes died, and obituaries in Honolulu printed his death and stated that the "inventor of the ukulele" had passed away. These publications were read and reprinted by other newspapers and reporters, eventually leading to wire services transmitting this news to the United States mainland. Newspapers, columnists, and magazines in cities like New York City, Boston, and Los Angeles, just to name a few, would reprint this somewhere in their publications. Whether it was a column here, a paragraph there, or any other fleeting mention, newspapers propagated further references to the ukulele. Additionally, newspaper headlines would emphasize the false fact that a white man had invented the ukulele, not a Native Hawaiian.

A Hawaiian girl with a ukulele, 1912. (Source: Public Domain, Bishop Museum)

Even as recent as the past two decades, misconceptions, uninformed criticisms, and myths about the ukulele continue to crop up. The "mini-guitar" enjoyed spikes of popularity during the period of the Roaring Twenties (1920-1929), the advent of postwar plastics, and the most recent surge in popularity, which was fueled by artists like Paul McCartney and Bruno Mars, along with thousands of online personalities on YouTube, Instagram, and other video platforms.

Hula

Although many people think of hula as a dance where exotic women wearing leis and grass skirts twirl and dance with their hips, the full scope of hula is much larger and more nuanced than the mainstream stereotype that has come to be associated with the word. Hula is an ancient form of dance, theater, and social and religious expression that traces its history to more than three hundred years ago. Hula has many legends and myths associated with its origins, with one example being that hula was the dance that Hiʻiaka, the sister of the goddess of fire and volcanoes, Pele, used to appease and calm her sister's hot temper. Hula is claimed to have been invented by different islands of Hawaiʻi, and these islands often have differing origin legends about the dance.

A promotional lobby card for an American romantic comedy film, Hula (1927). (Source: Paramount Pictures)

Hula can also be a visual dance form that accompanies a chant, called an *oli*, or a song, called a *mele*, where a story is told. Hula is the portrayal, dramatization, and acting out of the events and phenomena of the story. Like other traditional cultural dances around the world, hula is mostly danced by women and boasts a wide range of movements and routines, with most of them featuring a mostly stable upper body and a moving, bending lower body. Even though hula is typically performed by women, there are male hula dancers. In fact, it was considered a great honor to be an accomplished male hula dancer, as it was a sign that an individual would be a great warrior. The early Hawaiians, like other ancient cultures, believed that good dancers made good fighters.

Male Hula dancers in their performance costumes, 2017. (Source: Wikimedia Commons, TheRealAnthonySalerno)

In recent times, hula has seen a resurgence in academia and popular culture, especially with regards to competition and schooling. Hula-specific schools and groups come from all over Hawai'i to compete and display the most vibrant, rich, technical, and beautiful hula performances. In particular, the Merrie Monarch Festival is a week-long event that features many different facets of Hawaiian culture, including the most prestigious hula competition in the world. The festival honors King Kalakaua, who is credited with starting the First Hawaiian Renaissance and reinvigorating the lost arts and traditions of Hawai'i, especially hula.

Hula dancers practice for many years to compete, and they sport elaborate costumes with bands around their feet and hands that accentuate their movements and poses. Sometimes these bands are made out of decorated gourd rattles that shake and rattle as the dancer moves in rhythm with the beat of the percussion gourd that is traditionally used in hula, called an *ipu*.

Language

Although both English and Hawaiian are listed as Hawai'i's official languages, the vast majority of Hawaiians speak English, with less than 1 percent of Hawaiians being native speakers of Hawaiian. Even though Hawaiian is still an endangered language, it once was at the point of extinction due to the theological, educational, religious, and political pressures of Christian missionaries who arrived on Hawai'i many years ago. Luckily, King Kamehameha III reestablished the importance of the Hawaiian language and used it to encode the 1839 and 1840 Constitutions of the Hawaiian kingdom.

The Hawaiian language is a member of the Austronesian language family, and it is a Polynesian language. Lexical similarities, cognates, and comparative methods are able to linguistically prove the close relationships between Hawaiian and other Polynesian languages like Marquesan, Tahitian, Māori, and many more. These languages are not mutually intelligible but have basic word similarities and short phrases and utterances that can be understood between speakers of each language. Linguistic and genetic sampling that compares the level of comprehension and word similarity between languages supports the migratory and archaeological trends that predict the movements of ancient Polynesian people. Today, Hawaiian is taught in many schools, both public and private, and is maintained by different levels of academic institutions.

Although Hawaiians had no written language prior to Western contact, like many other cultures around the world, Hawaiian morphology and words adapt fairly well to the Latin script, partly because almost all Hawaiian words end in vowels. This writing system was adapted to the Hawaiian language by American Protestant missionaries, and they added consonants that were absent in the Native Hawaiian language to their alphabet. Although this newly made Hawaiian alphabet was close to one symbol per sound, it still did not allow foreign words to be easily introduced to Native Hawaiians, as the early missionaries were not aware of linguistic phenomena like phonotactics and morphological rules. In practice, many of these foreign words were Hawaiianized, and the remnants of this pattern can be seen in the Hawaiian language even today.

Hawaiian can be learned through a number of modern apps and online books, with language immersion being the most effective method of learning Hawaiian. The language follows the third most common word order of languages, the verb-subject-object word order, like Irish and Scottish Gaelic. Hawaiian also employs different forms of the word "we," distinguishing between the "inclusive we" that includes the person being spoken to and the "exclusive we" that excludes the person being spoken to. Hawaiian managed to escape suppression, especially after the overthrow of the Hawaiian kingdom, and experienced a revitalization along with other aspects of Hawaiian culture during the Hawaiian Renaissances.

Tourism and Popular Culture

Luau

Popularized by the surge of tourism in Hawai'i, a luau refers to a traditional Hawaiian feast and party that includes entertainment, music, and dance. Nowadays, the word has become synonymous with the word *party* and has been used as such in phrases like "a graduation luau,"

"a birthday luau," and "a wedding luau." In ancient times, due to the customs and rituals of *kapu*, men and women were not allowed to feast together and required separate areas for meals.

The luau has its roots as an *'aha'aina*, meaning a "gathering meal," where the serving of meat was the high point of the feast. Contrary to popular belief, meats and entire roasted pigs were not common in Native Hawaiian life, as this was not an abundant resource and was eaten only during special occasions. Nowadays, luau cuisine includes salmon, poke, roasted pigs, poi, beer, fruit cocktail, other roasted meats, and many other delicious dishes.

A tray of food served at a traditional Hawaiian luau featuring corn, yam, bacon, poi, and other side dishes. (Source: Wikimedia Commons, The Eloquent Peasant)

Luaus were "invented" by King Kamehameha II, who ended the *kapu* surrounding the events and held a feast where he ate alongside women in a symbolic gesture of new societal standards.

The word "luau" itself translates literally to "taro," and the feast takes this name because taro was one of the most common foods that were served at such feasts. Large open fires, clay pits, earthen ovens, and barbecue grills are often seen in luaus, where meat and other foods are prepared. Traditionally, utensils are not used in luaus, and all of the food is meant to be eaten by hand and in a communal setting. These gatherings would be a time for social bonding, collective celebration, bounty sharing, and as a form of religious ritual and thanksgiving. Luaus are often held by the beach or in specific purpose-built spots that are chosen for convenience, accessibility, cleanliness, comfort, and a nearby sunset view.

A photograph of Native Hawaiians at a luau, 1899. (Source: Our Islands and Their People, New York: Thompson Publishing Co.)

The rapid growth of the tourism industry saw luaus become a quintessential part of experiencing Hawai'i, as such events tied together many aspects of the islands. Luaus included Hawaiian music, Hawaiian cuisine, Hawaiian performances, and Hawaiian hospitality. Although some critics have written that the modern-day luau has become over-commercialized and, as a result, is divorced from its native roots and original meaning, the popularity of luaus has remained unaffected. The feasts can vary significantly and, thus, offer very different experiences, with factors including which island the luau is held on, the organizers of the luau, the seasonal availability of foods, and the extent to which the luau follows Native Hawaiian traditions. Nonetheless, luaus remain an extremely popular tourist experience where food, music, friends, and Native Hawaiian culture mix, and they will continue to thrive for the foreseeable future.

Lei

A lei is a Hawaiian and Polynesian garland that is usually worn around the neck and is a sign of honor, welcome, and friendship. Leis are made and given for a wide variety of reasons, with the most well-known instance being a welcome gift for travelers and tourists when they first arrive in Hawaiʻi. Besides that, leis are made and worn for hula performances, weddings, religious ceremonies, graduations, and school events. Historically, leis have been made and sold to newcomers since before World War II. Locals, along with wives and daughters of interracial marriages, would run stands selling leis, along with tropical fruits and snacks like cooked breadfruit, bananas, plantain fritters, pineapples, and the like. They would work at airports and the waterfront where passenger ships docked or embarked from the port.

Leis could be (and are traditionally still) made from flowers, beads, and seeds. There were stores that stocked lei flowers, beads, strings, tools, and seeds from collectors who sourced the beads and seeds that had washed down from the mountains of Hawaiʻi. Lei makers would drill holes in them and string them on cords and wires. Glass beads, seed hulls, and shells would also be used in certain leis, allowing leis to have an extremely diverse set of styles and looks.

Even paper leis had different types of folded and twisted styles. Some of the leis would incorporate sewing, back-sewing, special twisting techniques, and even knitting. Leis could be all sorts of colors or color combinations. Oral histories of lei makers show that they would take note of which styles and color schemes were most popular with foreigners or army men and make changes accordingly.

The hand of King Kamehameha's statue festooned with leis. The statue is located in Hawaii's Capital Historic District. (Source: Daniel Ramirez, Honolulu)

Lei sellers would crowd and show off their leis on their arms, trying to entice buyers and tourists because the business was a valuable supplementary source of income for their families. Many would use their backyards to grow different flowers, with some examples being Hawaiian hibiscus, crown flowers, plumerias, carnations, ilima, pikake jasmines, baldheads, and candle flowers. Luxurious and beautiful leis that are thick with real flowers can be immensely time-consuming to create by hand. Many lei makers have to pick certain flowers at specific times of the day, which means they invest lots of time into flower procurement and then even more time into stringing the flowers together. Since lei makers back in the 1800s and 1900s did not have the option of utilizing refrigeration to extend the shelf-life of their product, most leis would only last a few days unless other preservative measures were taken. Leis continue to be a central and prominent element of Hawaiian and Polynesian culture and aesthetics.

Hula girls wearing leis, some younger and some older, at Kapiolani Park, presumably all from the same halau *(school for learning hula). (Source: Wikimedia Commons, Hakilon)*

Conclusion

Summarily, there is much more to Hawai'i than meets the eye, from their awesome ancient navigating and sailing prowess to their lost great *heiaus* of yore. Hawai'i has always been and will very likely continue to be a unique and important point of interest for the entire Pacific Rim and the ocean itself. We are only now beginning to see the beauty and diversity that such an island nation offers in terms of island hopping, coral reefs, migration patterns, and multiclimate environments. Hawai'i is an ecological treasure that is rare, isolated, and more vulnerable than people are aware of. This book is just one small step in raising awareness of the precarious nature that, sadly, many island nations face in terms of their future ecological stability.

Hawai'i has taken this geographical and natural richness and supplied it with a narrative that is equally as rich and detailed. Their ancient mythologies and ideologies are quite unlike any other in the world, arising in a history almost devoid of wider civilizational influences. Its people have faced enormous historical challenges, from oppression and annexation all the way to germ-driven genocide. Fortunately, its people have survived and are uncovering their deep roots, an effort that is gaining traction. From its royal lineages and families of gods, Hawai'i's people have much to look forward to. They have even more to share with the world, as its famous peoples and artifacts have already proven to inspire and create change throughout the world. Undoubtedly, its future is fertile and almost unfailingly positive if Hawai'i's politics, government, and socioeconomics serve its people.

Although this book touched upon most of Hawai'i's finest moments and times of trouble, we hope that our reader takes with them a sense of wonder, hunger, and joy and learn more about one of the world's most hidden gems nestled in the middle of the Pacific Ocean. If you ever visit the archipelago of Hawai'i, we hope that this book will provide you with an awareness and an understanding of the stories that run through the lands and imbue it with *mana*, the spiritual energy and life force that runs through its people. Hawaii was, is, and will very likely continue to be a beautiful place of deep import, and we hope to have shared a bit of that beauty with you through our writing.

Here's another book by Captivating History that you might like

Free Bonus from Captivating History (Available for a Limited time)

Hi History Lovers!

Now you have a chance to join our exclusive history list so you can get your first history ebook for free as well as discounts and a potential to get more history books for free! Simply visit the link below to join.

Captivatinghistory.com/ebook

Also, make sure to follow us on Facebook, Twitter and Youtube by searching for Captivating History.

References

Michi Kodama-Nishimoto. *Talking Hawai'i's Story: Oral Histories of an Island People.* 2009.

Jim Tranquada & John King. *The 'Ukulele: A History.* 2012.

Edward D. Beechert. *Working in Hawai'i: A Labor History.* 1985.

William D. Westervelt. *Legends of Gods and Ghosts.* 1915.

Martha Beckwith. *Hawaiian Mythology.* 1940.

William DeWitt Alexanders. *A Brief History of the Hawaiian People.* 1891.

Robert P. Dye & Bob Dye. *Hawai'i Chronicles: World War Two in Hawai'i.* University of Hawai'i Press. 2000.

Jon Thares. *Hawai'i at the Crossroads of the U.S. and Japan before the Pacific War.* 2008.

Alan C. Ziegler. *Hawaiian Natural History, Ecology and Evolution.* 2002.

Noenoe K. Silva. *Reconstructing Native Hawaiian Intellectual History.* 2017.

Dan Cisco. *Hawai'i Sports, History, Facts and Statistics.* 1999. Haunani-Kay Trask. *From a Native Daughter.* 1993.

Jon Van Dyke. *Who Owns the Crown Lands of Hawai'i?* 2007.

Christopher Grandy. *Hawai'i Becalmed, Economic Lessons of the 1990s.* 2002.

Daniel Marston. *The Pacific War Companion: From Pearl Harbor to Hiroshima.* 2003.

Tom Dye. "Population Trends in Hawai'i before 1778." The Hawaiian Journal of History. 1994.

Carol A. MacLennan. *Hawai'i Turns to Sugar: The Rise of Plantation Centers.* 1997.

Ronald Takaki. *Raising Cane: The World of Plantation Hawai'i.* 1994.

Oswald Bushnell. *The Gifts of Civilization: Germs and Genocide in Hawai'i.* 1993.

Dan Boylan, T. Michael Holmes. *John A. Burns: The Man and His Times.* 2000.

Kanalu Terry Young. *Rethinking the Native Hawaiian Past.* 1998.

Mahealani Uchiyama. *The Haumana Hula Handbook for Students of Hawaiian Dance.* 2016.

Rick Carroll. *IZ: Voice of the People.* 2006.

David Davis. *Waterman: The Life and Times of Duke Kahanamoku.* 2015.

http://www.hawaiihistory.org/index.cfm?CategoryID=311&fuseaction=ig.page – Accessed: 01/16/2022

https://oceanservice.noaa.gov/facts/hawaii.html - Accessed: 01/16/2022

https://books.google.co.uk/books?id=uuMwvd9S5GwC&pg=PA4&redir_esc=y#v=onepage&q&f=false Accessed: 01/16/2022

https://www.smithsonianmag.com/travel/what-were-still-learning-about-hawaii-74730/ -

Accessed: 01/16/2022

https://teara.govt.nz/en/pacific-migrations/page-3 - Accessed: 01/16/2022

https://www.zealandtattoo.co.nz/tattoo-styles/polynesian-tattoo-history-meanings-traditional-designs/ - Accessed: 01/16/2022

https://www.hilohattie.com/blogs/news/the-creation-of-the-hawaiian-islands - Accessed:

01/17/2022

http://www.hawaiihistory.org/index.cfm?fuseaction=ig.page&PageID=383 - Accessed:

01/15/2022

https://www.mauimagazine.net/in-praise-of-wahine/ - Accessed: 01/15/2022

https://prezi.com/delblsr6zq2r/ancient-hawaiian-tools/ - Accessed: 01/17/2022

https://www.mauimagazine.net/hawaiian-weapons/4/ - Accessed: 01/17/2022

https://www.history.com/this-day-in-history/cook-discovers-hawaii - Accessed: 01/15/2022

https://www.nps.gov/puhe/learn/historyculture/kamehameha.htm - Accessed: 01/17/2022

https://www.pandaonline.com/ancient-hawaiian-lifestyle/ - Accessed: 01/06/2022

https://www.hawaiiankingdom.org/political-history.shtml - Accessed: 01/06/2022

Sally Engle Merry (2000). *Colonizing Hawai'i: The Cultural Power of Law*. Princeton University Press. p. 76. ISBN 0-691-00932-5.

Richard H. Kosaki (1978). "Constitutions and Constitutional Conventions of Hawaii". *Hawaiian Journal of History*. 12. Hawaii Historical Society. pp. 120–138. hdl:10524/196

https://www.digitalhistory.uh.edu/disp_textbook.cfm?smtid=3&psid=12 - Accessed: 01/06/2022

https://www.google.com/maps/place/Thomas+Square/@21.3026278,-157.8513258,17z/data=!3m1!4b1!4m5!3m4!1s0x7c006de71c2d8ad1:0x2bfcaaf702330256!8m2!3d21.3026278!4d-157.8491371?hl=en - Accessed: 01/06/2022

https://www.honolulu.gov/rep/site/ocs/roh/ROHChapter16a12.pdf - Accessed: 01/06/2022

https://law-hawaii.libguides.com/c.php?g=125440&p=1443600 - Accessed: 01/02/2022

https://www.gohawaii.com/islands/hawaii-big-island/regions/kohala - Accessed: 12/22/2021

https://www.nationalarchives.gov.uk/education/resources/captain-cook-in-hawaii/ - Accessed: 12/22/2021

https://www.hilohattie.com/blogs/news/the-creation-of-the-hawaiian-islands - Accessed: 12/22/2021

https://www.mauimagazine.net/in-praise-of-wahine/ - Accessed: 12/22/2022

https://luaus.org/elements-of-a-luau-taro-in-hawaiian-culture/ - Accessed: 12/21/2021

http://www2.hawaii.edu/~dhonda/ahupua'a.htm - Accessed: 12/21/2021

https://www.smithsonianmag.com/travel/hawaii-history-and-heritage-4164590/ Accessed: 12/15/2021

https://moneyweek.com/428138/25-february-1843-hawaii-occupied-during-the-paulet-affair/ - Accessed: 12/14/2021 https://www.gohawaii.com/hawaiian-culture/history Accessed: 12/14/2021

https://www.tourmaui.com/wp-content/uploads/Maui-History-Engraving-American-Boat-Hawaiians-in-Canoe.jpg Accessed: 12/13/2021

https://historichawaii.org/2020/06/19/bicentennial-of-the-arrival-of-abmc-missionaries-and-establishment-of-three-historic-churches/ Accessed: 12/13/2021

https://www.history.com/topics/us-states/hawaii Accessed: 12/13/2021

http://www.islandbreath.org/hawaiinei/hawaiinei.html Accessed: 12/13/2021

https://www.freehawaii.org/ Accessed: 12/13/2021

http://libweb.hawaii.edu/digicoll/annexation/annexation.php Accessed: 12/13/2021

http://www.hawaiiplantationvillage.org/ Accessed: 12/13/2021

http://www.coffeetimes.com/henry.htm Accessed: 12/13/2021

https://books.google.co.uk/books?id=jbBvWQ8LGKEC&pg=PA220&redir_esc=y Accessed: 12/13/2021

Alexander, Arthur (1937), *Koloa Plantation 1835 - 1935*, Honolulu, HI Accessed: 12/13/2021

https://encyclopedia.densho.org/Plantations/ Accessed: 12/13/2021

https://morganreport.org/mediawiki/index.php?title=Kingdom_of_Hawaii_Constitution_of_1839 Accessed: 12/13/2021

https://www.familysearch.org/wiki/en/Hawaii,_United_States_Genealogy - Accessed: 12/11/2021

https://www.britannica.com/topic/Hawaiian - Accessed: 12/11/2021

https://books.google.co.uk/books?id=KTNLx2gHMxIC&pg=PA239&redir_esc=y Accessed: 12/11/2021

https://www.pandaonline.com/hawaiian-taro/ Accessed: 11/10/2021

http://hawaii-guide.info/past.and.present/history/polynesians.arrive/ - Accessed: 11/10/2021

http://hawaii-guide.info/past.and.present/history/polynesians.arrive/ - Accessed: 11/05/2021

https://em.gohawaii.com/mtr40/custom/prod/plannerorder/planner_step1.php?bureau=hvcb - Accessed: 11/05/2021

http://www.hawaii.edu/PCSS/biblio/articles/2000to2004/2004-sexual-behavior-in-pre-contact-hawaii.html Accessed: 1/23/2022